THE

EVERYTHING KIDS'®

Knock Knock Book

Jokes guaranteed to leave your friends in stitches

Aileen Weintraub

Adams Media
Avon, Massachusetts

To Chris, WHO's always THERE. Aardvark a million miles for you.

EDITORIAL
Publishing Director: Gary M. Krebs
Managing Editor: Kate McBride
Copy Chief: Laura MacLaughlin
Acquisitions Editor: Bethany Brown
Development Editor: Julie Gutin
Production Editor: Jamie Wielgus

PRODUCTION
Production Director: Susan Beale
Production Manager: Michelle Roy Kelly
Series Designer: Colleen Cunningham
Layout and Graphics: Colleen Cunningham,
  Rachael Eiben, John Paulhus,
  Daria Perreault, Erin Ring
Cover Layout: Paul Beatrice, Frank Rivera

An Everything® Series Book.
Everything® is a registered trademark of F & W Publications, Inc.

Published by Adams Media, an F & W Publications Company
57 Littlefield Street, Avon, MA 02322. U.S.A.
www.adamsmedia.com

ISBN: 1-59337-127-6

Printed in the United States of America.

J   I   H   G   F   E   D   C   B   A

Cover illustrations by Dana Regan.
Interior illustrations by Kurt Dolber and Barry Littmann.
Puzzles by Beth Blair.

Puzzle Power Software by Centron Software Technologies, Inc., was used to create puzzle grids.

This book is available at quantity discounts for bulk purchases.
For information, call 1-800-872-5627.

See the entire Everything® series at *www.everything.com*.

Acknowledgments

First and foremost, I'd like to thank the people at Adams for all their hard work, including Kate McBride, Bethany Brown, Julie Gutin, Kate Petrella, Laura MacLaughlin, Jamie Wielgus, Erin Ring, and everyone else who worked on this project. Without their dedication, this book would not be possible. I'd also like to thank Joyce Romano.

I want to express gratitude to my mother for her support and encouragement throughout my career. And to Alex and Ryan who will bring many years of inspiration and happiness. Also to Amanda Powell, who just flat out makes me laugh.

Knock knock!
Who's there?
Keith.
Keith who?
Keith a positive attitude!

Knock knock!
Who's there?
Otis.
Otis who?
Otis a beautiful day!

Contents

Introduction

Can you think of anything more inviting than a good knock-knock joke? Who can resist answering "who's there?" after hearing someone say "knock knock"? You'd be hard-pressed to find someone who doesn't love these jokes.

Knock-knocks are popular in every country where people speak English, including the United States, Canada, Great Britain, and Australia. That's because each knock-knock joke is a pun, or a play on words, and puns are more popular in English than they are in other languages.

So, what's the purpose of a knock-knock joke anyway? Well, that's easy! To make you laugh, of course! A good laugh can have many truly wonderful results. Laughter is a universal language that all humans share no matter where they live or how old they are. Laughter can connect people of all ages around the world. Did you know that babies start laughing when they're only two months old? That's so much earlier than speaking or even crawling. Babies know funny when they see or hear it. And so do the rest of us.

Another fabulous result of a good laugh is that it really *is* the best medicine. Laughter is a great cure when you're down in the dumps and just can't shake the blues. Even the experts agree: Laughter helps to keep us healthy and happy. Science shows us that laughter increases the amount of oxygen running through our blood, makes us relax, and helps us feel less nervous during stressful times. This is no secret. People have known this for centuries. Some people even make a living just getting others to laugh!

Back in the very old days, court jesters appeared before the king and queen just to amuse them. Today, comedians, clowns, actors, and actresses all work hard to come up with funny material to get a good laugh from their audiences. Sometimes people will go out of their way to find something that will make them laugh. They watch movies, go to the theater, and turn on the television set, all in the hopes of kicking back and seeing how funny life can be!

Laughter makes people happy, and we all know that everybody likes to be around happy people. So crack open this book and start chuckling, giggling, guffawing, or even rolling-on-the-floor belly laughing. Gather some friends and start your own hysterical society. This is a group that gets together to tell each other jokes, riddles, and rhymes, act silly, and just plain make each other laugh. Don't worry if no one's laughing right away. Laughter is contagious. Just start tee-heeing, ho-ho-ing, and ha-ha-ing, and everyone else will soon follow.

Knock knock!
Who's there?
Hal.
Hal who?
Hal me tight!

Knock knock!
Who's there?
Hank.
Hank who?
Hank you!

Knock knock!
Who's there?
Erma.
Erma who?
Erma going tell you lots of knock-knock jokes!

Knock knock!
Who's there?
Heifer.
Heifer who?
Heifer dollar is better than none!

Knock knock!
Who's there?
Scold.
Scold who?
'Scold out!

Knock knock!
Who's there?
Lettuce.
Lettuce who?
Lettuce in and I'll tell you!

Knock knock!
Who's there?
Doug.
Doug who?
Doug-out is where the baseball
    players sit!

What am I?

I have a very big mouth, but I never say a word. I have a bank, but I don't keep any money in it. I have a bed, but I never get tired. I wave at everybody, but I have no hands. **What am I?**

A river

Knock knock!
Who's there?
Abe Lincoln.
Abe Lincoln who?
A-be Lincoln light on a Christmas tree!

Knock knock!
Who's there?
Barbie.
Barbie who?
Barbie Q chicken!

Knock knock!
Who's there?
Gumby.
Gumby who?
Gumby our guest for dinner!

Fun Fact

Don't Sweat It
Did you know that there are more chickens than people in the world? That's because chickens can lay about 320 eggs each year. Also, did you know that chickens never sweat? They have to spread their wings and pant in order to keep cool.

Try This

Crawly Caterpillars
Make caterpillars out of old toilet paper rolls! Wrap the toilet paper roll in colorful construction paper (you can use tape or glue to make sure it sticks). Color squiggly designs on it. Cut up a pipe cleaner into six one-inch pieces. Glue or stick the pieces through the bottom of the caterpillar for legs. Now cut another pipe cleaner in half and bend the halves in the shape of antennae. Glue the antennae to the top of the caterpillar's head. Find a pompon and glue it on for a nose. Draw on some eyes. For extra big caterpillars, use old paper towel rolls instead!

Knock knock!
Who's there?
Jude.
Jude who?
Jude the food, then swallowed it!

Knock knock!
Who's there?
Icy.
Icy who?
Icy a big monster under the bed!

Knock knock!
Who's there?
Window.
Window who?
Window we get to play something else?

Knock knock!
Who's there?
Agatha.
Agatha who?
Agatha the chills when it's cold!

comedian:

A man or a woman who makes a living by being funny. It is a comedian's job to tell jokes and get people giggling.

Knock knock!
Who's there?
Howell.
Howell who?
Howell do you know me?

Knock knock!
Who's there?
Genoa.
Genoa who?
Genoa good dentist?

Knock knock!
Who's there?
Xavier.
Xavier who?
Xavier money in the bank!

Knock knock!
Who's there?
Ham.
Ham who?
Ham I going to see you again?

Knock knock!
Who's there?
Cargo.
Cargo who?
Car-go vroom vroom!

Knock knock!
Who's there?
Thelonius.
Thelonius who?
Thelonius night of the week!

Knock knock!

Who's there?

Watson.

Watson who?

Watson television?

Knock knock!

Who's there?

Lionel.

Lionel who?

Lionel eat you if he's hungry!

What's So Funny

Knock knock!

Who's there?

Leaf.

Leaf who?

Leaf me alone!

Noah

Knock, knock.

Who's there?

Noah.

Noah who?

Use the decoder to find the answer!

SURPRISE

N O A h

D O S E N t   k n o w   y o u

EithER

What's So Funny

HA HA HA HA HA HA

Knock knock!
Who's there?
Court.
Court who?
Court of milk!

Knock knock!
Who's there?
Teresa.
Teresa who?
Teresa fly in my soup!

Knock knock!
Who's there?
Dishwasher.
Dishwasher who?
Dishwasher the way I always shpoke!

Knock knock!
Who's there?
Giza.
Giza who?
Giza nice man!

Knock knock!
Who's there?
Stopwatch.
Stopwatch who?
Stopwatch you're doing!

Fun Fact

English All Over
There are many countries that have English-speaking people. In many countries where English is not the first language, English is taught in schools. Did you know that there are more English-speaking people in China than there are in the United States?

Knock knock!
Who's there?
Founder.
Founder who?
Founder book in the
   library!

Knocked to Pieces

A knock-knock and its answer were put into the large grid, and then cut into eight pieces. See if you can figure out where each piece goes, and write the letters in their proper places. When you have filled in the grid correctly, you will be able to read the joke from left to right, and top to bottom.

HINT: The black boxes stand for the spaces between words. Careful—some pieces are turned or flipped!

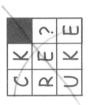

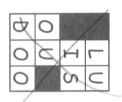

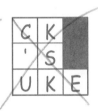

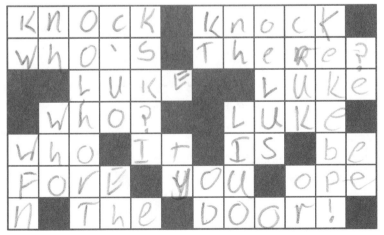
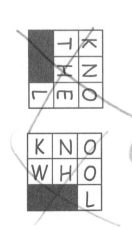

Say What?

To find the end to this knock-knock, cross out all letters that follow these rules:

- sound like the name of a vegetable
- come after "L" in the alphabet
- are tenth in the alphabet

When you are finished, read the remaining letters from left to right, and top to bottom.

Knock, knock.

Who's there?

Lena!

Lena who?

R M L J E P N M A M J
L J I M P T M T P L E
C J P L M J O J M J P
J M S J M E P J R J M
P A J N J D P J M J I
M P W M I P M L J P L
T J E P M L P M J L P M
P Y M O M P M U J M J

Lena Little close and will tell you

I can't Hear You

These two whispering girls may look the same, but see if you can find the ten differences between them.

HINT: It doesn't count that they are facing in different directions.

8

Knock knock!
Who's there?
Dewey.
Dewey who?
Dewey have to stay much longer?

Knock knock!
Who's there?
Samuel.
Samuel who?
Samuel like and Samuel won't!

witty:
Something that is clever or amusing. A witty statement will impress people or give them a good chuckle.

Words to Know

Try This

Masked and Whiskered

Make a cat mask! Cut a paper plate in half, and use one half for your mask, so that the curved edge of the plate is at the top of the mask. Cut out two triangles for your eyes and a triangle for your nose. Glue three pipe cleaners on each side of the nose for whiskers. Cut ears out of construction paper and glue them on top. Then punch a hole through the sides of the mask and thread some yarn around it so you can tie it to your head. And don't forget to add decorations!

Knock knock!
Who's there?
Yoga.
Yoga who?
Yo-ga what it takes to be the best!

Knock knock!
Who's there?
Camel.
Camel who?
Camel get it, dinner's ready!

Knock knock!
Who's there?
Milton.
Milton who?
Milton snow turns to water!

Knock knock!
Who's there?
Freeze.
Freeze who?
Freeze a jolly good fella!

Knock knock!
Who's there?
Tex.
Tex who?
Tex two to tango!

Knock knock!
Who's there?
Aardvark.
Aardvark who?
Aardvark a million miles for you!

Try This

Home Sweet Home
What could be sweeter than a house made of candy? Gather some soft candy such as gumdrops, marshmallows, and gummy shapes. Get a box of toothpicks and start building! Think of the candies as corners and toothpicks as edges, and build by sticking toothpicks through the candies to connect them. You can start with a triangle or square and keep building up. Just don't eat the whole house all at once!

Knock knock!
Who's there?
Fletcher.
Fletcher who?
Fletcher in or she'll break down the door!

Knock knock!
Who's there?
Vic.
Vic who?
Vic some flowers for me!

Knock knock!
Who's there?
Izzie.
Izzie who?
Izzie going to tell any more jokes?

Knock knock!
Who's there?
Sherwood.
Sherwood who?
Sherwood like some more pie!

Knock knock!
Who's there?
Bacon.
Bacon who?
Bacon a cake for the party!

Knock knock!
Who's there?
Bertha.
Bertha who?
Bertha-day party!

Knock knock!
Who's there?
Howl.
Howl who?
Howl I know if you're on your way over?

Knock knock!
Who's there?
Tail.
Tail who?
Tail all your friends about it!

Knock knock!
Who's there?
Adlai.
Adlai who?
Adlai my life on the line!

What am I?

I can grow up to 19 feet tall. I often weigh more than 1,600 pounds, and I can clean my ears with my 21-inch-long tongue. Even though I am so big and tall, I am a gentle creature and can be found roaming the African savanna.
What am I?

A giraffe

Knock knock!
Who's there?
Rabbit.
Rabbit who?
Rabbit up carefully, it's a present!

Knock knock!
Who's there?
House.
House who?
House it going?

Knock knock!
Who's there?
Wheel.
Wheel who?
Wheel stop coming over
if we're not invited!

pun:

Words to Know

A word or joke that is a play on words and may have two or more meanings. All knock-knock jokes are puns.

Knock knock!
Who's there?
Maine.
Maine who?
Maine thing here is that we're all friends!

Knock knock!
Who's there?
Thermos.
Thermos who?
Thermos be another way!

Knock knock!
Who's there?
Statue.
Statue who?
Statue or is that someone else?

12

Chapter 2
When Fun Comes a Knockin'

What am I?

I am a tree or shrub that grows along the edge of streams and beaver ponds. My roots spread out and grow deep. They keep the soil from getting washed away by floods.
What am I?

A willow

Knock knock!
Who's there?
Ears.
Ears who?
Ears some more knock-knock jokes
for you!

Knock knock!
Who's there?
Feline.
Feline who?
Feline fine, and you?

Knock knock!
Who's there?
Tad.
Tad who?
Tad old black magic!

Knock knock!
Who's there?
Freddie.
Freddie who?
Freddie cat, Freddie cat!

Knock knock!
Who's there?
Eisenhower.
Eisenhower who?
Eisenhower late getting here!

Knock knock!
Who's there?
Sheik.
Sheik who?
Sheik-speare was a famous poet!

Try This

A Quick Trick

Put an ice cube in a bowl of water. Lower a string on top of the ice cube. Sprinkle salt on top of the ice cube and the string. Then try to lift the ice cube with the string. The salt will melt just enough ice so the string will stick.

Knock knock!
Who's there?
Burma.
Burma who?
Burma hand on the stove!

Knock knock!
Who's there?
Ostrich.
Ostrich who?
Ostrich my arms up to the sky!

Knock knock!
Who's there?
Beagle.
Beagle who?
Beagle with lox!

Knock knock!
Who's there?
Lena.
Lena who?
Lena little closer, I have something to tell you!

Knock knock!
Who's there?
Pooch.
Pooch who?
Pooch your coat on!

Knock knock!
Who's there?
Hurley.
Hurley who?
Hurley to bed, Hurley to rise!

What's So Funny

Knock knock!
Who's there?
Weavish.
Weavish who?
Weavish you a very happy birthday!

Mix and Match

Write the number of the correct ending into the space by each
knock knock. Choose from the list at the bottom of the page.

KNOCK, KNOCK.
Who's there?
BOO.
Boo who?

KNOCK, KNOCK.
Who's there?
CASH.
Cash who?

KNOCK, KNOCK.
Who's there?
COWS.
Cows who?

KNOCK, KNOCK.
Who's there?
ATCH.
Atch who?

KNOCK, KNOCK.
Who's there?
YOU.
You who?

KNOCK, KNOCK.
Who's there?
YA.
Ya who?

1. Don't cry — it's only a joke!
2. No they don't. Owls who!
3. I'm glad you're having a good time!
4. I always knew you were nuts!
5. Oh, I'm sorry you have a cold!
6. Who are you calling?

Knock knock!
Who's there?
Poker.
Poker who?
Poker and see if
she gets upset!

Knock knock!
Who's there?
Iran.
Iran who?
Iran as fast as I can!

Knock knock!
Who's there?
Justin.
Justin who?
Justin time for dinner!

Knock knock!
Who's there?
Omelet.
Omelet who?
Om-e-let stronger than you think!

Knock knock!
Who's there?
Megan.
Megan who?
Megan supper for you!

Knock knock!
Who's there?
Nicholas.
Nicholas who?
Nicholas equal to five cents!

Knock knock!
Who's there?
Havana.
Havana who?
Havan-a nice time!

funnyman:

Words to Know

A funnyman is just that, a man who is funny. Sometimes a comedian will be introduced to his audience with this title. One famous funnyman is Robin Williams. Of course, there are funnywomen too!

Knock knock!
Who's there?
Shirley.
Shirley who?
Shirley you don't want
    to hear any more jokes!

Knock knock!
Who's there?
Miri.
Miri who?
Miri me and we'll spend the rest of our
    lives together!

What's So Funny

Knock knock!
Who's there?
Passover.
Passover who?
Passover that chapter,
it's boring!

Knock knock!
Who's there?
Uganda.
Uganda who?
Uganda keep getting away with this!

Knock knock!
Who's there?
Yachts.
Yachts who?
Yachts up with you?

Fun Fact

A Smelly Situation!
The power of smell is
fascinating. This sense is very
important to our survival. For
example, it lets us know whether the food we're
about to eat is fresh or spoiled. In all, the human
nose can identify more than 10,000 different
smells.

Knock knock!
Who's there?
Irma.
Irma who?
Irma great student!

Knock knock!
Who's there?
Genoa.
Genoa who?
Genoa any new knock-knock jokes?

Knock knock!
Who's there?
Dent.
Dent who?
Dent be late!

Knock knock!
Who's there?
Gorilla.
Gorilla who?
Gorilla my dreams!

Knock knock!
Who's there?
Ya.
Ya who?
When did you
    become a cowboy?

Knock knock!
Who's there?
Berlin.
Berlin who?
Berlin' the water for some tea!

Knock knock!
Who's there?
Ayn.
Ayn who?
Ayn on my way!

Knock knock!
Who's there?
Nixon.
Nixon who?
Nixon stones will break my bones!

What am I?

I live underground in dry fields. I don't like to be around people at all. I'm very small, but I sure am tough and will defend my territory.
What am I?

A badger

19

Knock knock!
Who's there?
Detail.
Detail who?
De-tail on de rabbit is fluffy!

Knock knock!
Who's there?
Fodder.
Fodder who?
Fodder and I are going to the park!

Knock knock!
Who's there?
Fanta.
Fanta who?
Fanta Claus!

Knock knock!
Who's there?
Boo.
Boo who?
Don't cry, it's
   just a joke!

Try This

Butterflies Welcome!
Make a butterfly garden. There are more than 10,000 types of butterflies in the world. They all flock to certain kinds of plants. If you have those plants in your garden, you'll surely see butterflies. Late spring or early summer is the best time to plant. Try milkweed for monarchs. Butterfly bush and butterfly weed also are great. See how many other butterfly plants you can find!

Knock knock!
Who's there?
Uruguay.
Uruguay who?
You go Uruguay, and I'll go mine!

Knock knock!
Who's there?
Affer.
Affer who?
Affer got!

20

Knock knock!
Who's there?
Hurda.
Hurda who?
Hurda my finger in the door!

Knock knock!
Who's there?
Costa.
Costa who?
Costa lot of money!

Knock knock!
Who's there?
Fiddle.
Fiddle who?
'Fiddle make you feel better, I'll tell you!

Knock knock!
Who's there?
Kook.
Kook who?
You sound like a cuckoo!

Knock knock!
Who's there?
Camilla.
Camilla who?
Camill-a little squirt!

Fifi is my best helper!

Please Fix That

The letters in each column go in the squares directly below them, but not in the same order! Black squares are for punctuation, and the spaces between the words. When you have correctly filled in the grid, you will have a silly answer from Mr. Fix It!

Knock, knock.
Who's there?
Poodle.
Poodle who?

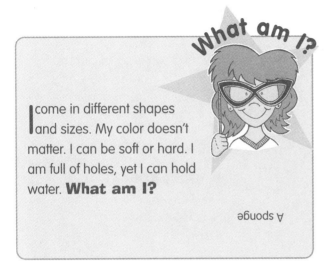

What am I?

I come in different shapes and sizes. My color doesn't matter. I can be soft or hard. I am full of holes, yet I can hold water. **What am I?**

A sponge

Knock knock!
Who's there?
Dublin.
Dublin who?
Dublin the bus fare!

Knock knock!
Who's there?
Asthma.
Asthma who?
Asthma anything you want!

Knock knock!
Who's there?
Justice.
Justice who?
Just-ice time, but that's it!

Knock knock!
Who's there?
Usher.
Usher who?
Usher wish we could do something else!

Knock knock!
Who's there?
Ghana.
Ghana who?
Ghana dance all night!

Knock knock!
Who's there?
Pear.
Pear who?
Pear of earrings!

Knock knock!
Who's there?
Sue.
Sue who?
Sue prize!

What's So Funny

Knock knock!
Who's there?
Bonn.
Bonn who?
Bonn on the
Fourth of July!

Knock knock!
Who's there?
Saul.
Saul who?
'Saul in the name of love!

Knock knock!
Who's there?
Wilma.
Wilma who?
Wilma lunch be ready soon?

Knock knock!
Who's there?
Eclipse.
Eclipse who?
Eclipse my toenails!

Knock knock!
Who's there?
Parkway.
Parkway who?
Parkway over there!

Knock knock!
Who's there?
Udder.
Udder who?
Udder madness!

Fun Fact

Don't Bother Trying!
Your elbow is a very important
part of your body. It is the joint
between the upper and lower arm.
Your elbow allows your arm to bend. Without
elbows, we would have a very hard time carrying
out many basic tasks. But did you know that it is
impossible to lick your own elbows? (I'll bet you
tried to anyway!)

Knock knock!
Who's there?
Norway.
Norway who?
Norway am I leaving this house!

Hidden Helper

The answer to this joke is hidden in the letter grid. Use these clues to help figure it out:

- The answer starts in a corner.
- You read the answer in a logical order, one word after the other.
- You must add the punctuation.

Knock, knock.

Who's there?

E	R	L	L	E	B	R
P	E	B	R	O	O	O
A	L	N	E	K	D	O
I	L	L	G	O	R	D
R	B	O	N	R	U	E
M	E	E	N	B	O	H
A	N	H	A	S	Y	T

That's all I hear all day — knock, knock, knock!

21

Ring Again

JOE

Knock knock!
Who's there?
Alfie.
Alfie who?
Alfie horrible if you go!

Knock knock!
Who's there?
Walt.
Walt who?
Walt you don't know won't hurt you!

Knock knock!
Who's there?
Ewen.
Ewen who?
Ewen me could make great music!

Knock knock!
Who's there?
Amusing.
Amusing who?
Am-using my new joke book!

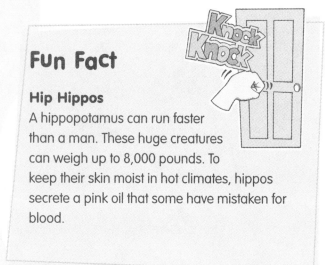

Fun Fact

Hip Hippos

A hippopotamus can run faster than a man. These huge creatures can weigh up to 8,000 pounds. To keep their skin moist in hot climates, hippos secrete a pink oil that some have mistaken for blood.

Knock knock!
Who's there?
Centaur.
Centaur who?
Cent-aur out for some more pizza!

Knock knock!
Who's there?
Aldus.
Aldus who?
Aldus fuss for nothing!

Knock knock!
Who's there?
Leslie.
Leslie who?
Leslie before anyone sees us!

Knock knock!
Who's there?
Stella.
Stella who?
Stella nobody's home!

Knock knock!
Who's there?
Aloha.
Aloha who?
Aloha you the rope!

Knock knock!
Who's there?
Wayne.
Wayne who?
Wayne keeps falling on my head,
    so I bought an umbwella!

Knock knock!
Who's there?
Shel.
Shel who?
Shel be coming 'round the mountain!

Knock knock!
Who's there?
Jack.
Jack who?
Jack of all trades!

Knock knock!
Who's there?
Locker.
Locker who?
Locker up for what she's done!

Knock knock!
Who's there?
Quack.
Quack who?
Quack another bad joke and I'm
    leaving!

Knock knock!
Who's there?
Gabe.
Gabe who?
Gabe it everything I got!

Knock knock!
Who's there?
Jubilee.
Jubilee who?
Jubilee in magic?

Knock knock!
Who's there?
Farmer.
Farmer who?
Farmer birthday I'm getting a new bike!

Knock knock!
Who's there?
Diploma.
Diploma who?
Diploma came to fix the toilet!

Chapter 3

Tied Up in Knock-Knocks

Fun Fact

Amazing Snails

Snails are very interesting creatures, but most of the time we don't even notice them. That's because they are often underground, they move very slowly, and they don't make much noise. But did you know that many snails can lift things that weigh 10 times more than their bodies do? They also can sleep for three years at a time.

Knock knock!
Who's there?
Zany.
Zany who?
Zany body home?

Knock knock!
Who's there?
Figs.
Figs who?
Figs the chair, it broke!

Knock knock!
Who's there?
Willy.
Willy who?
Willy call me before he comes over?

Knock knock!
Who's there?
Thumb.
Thumb who?
Thumb body is at the door!

Knock knock!
Who's there?
Rover.
Rover who?
Rover hill, Rover dale!

Knock knock!
Who's there?
Felix.
Felix who?
'Felix my ice cream, I'll be upset!

Knock knock!
Who's there?
Vet.
Vet who?
Vet are you going to do today?

Knock knock!
Who's there?
Steven.
Steven who?
Steven the walls have ears!

Knock knock!
Who's there?
Evelyn.
Evelyn who?
Evelyn comes full circle!

Knock knock!
Who's there?
Datsun.
Datsun who?
Datsun old one!

Knock knock!
Who's there?
Emma.
Emma who?
Emma 'fraid I have to go home now!

Knock knock!
Who's there?
Havana.
Havana who?
Havan-a great time, hope you are too!

Knock knock!
Who's there?
De Witt.
De Witt who?
De Witt now!

Knock knock!
Who's there?
Dozen.
Dozen who?
Dozen anyone know?

Knock knock!
Who's there?
Antilles.
Antilles who?
Antilles comes home,
we just have to wait!

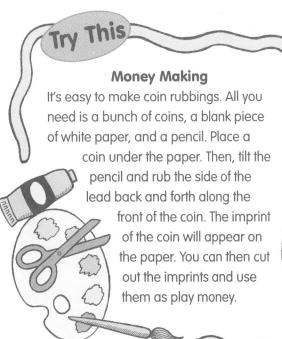

Knock knock!
Who's there?
Alfred.
Alfred who?
Alfred of monsters? Not me!

Knock knock!
Who's there?
Little old lady.
Little old lady who?
I didn't know you could yodel!

Knock knock!
Who's there?
Pierre.
Pierre who?
Pierre through the telescope!

Knock knock!
Who's there?
Albert.
Albert who?
Al-bert you don't know who this is!

Knock knock!
Who's there?
Honda.
Honda who?
Honda road again!

Knock knock!
Who's there?
Oliver.
Oliver who?
Oliver 'nother
    cookie please!

Try This

Money Making

It's easy to make coin rubbings. All you need is a bunch of coins, a blank piece of white paper, and a pencil. Place a coin under the paper. Then, tilt the pencil and rub the side of the lead back and forth along the front of the coin. The imprint of the coin will appear on the paper. You can then cut out the imprints and use them as play money.

Alli-ooPS!

Start at number 1 and connect the dots in order to find the answer to this joke. But be careful—you may not want to answer the door when you see who is knocking!

Knock, knock.

Who's there?

Alli.

Alli who?

Knock knock!
Who's there?
Gipper.
Gipper who?
Gipper a hand!

hilarious:

Something that makes you laugh so hard you can't control yourself. You just keep laughing and laughing. Anything or anyone can be hilarious!

Words to Know

How Polite!

Swim through the tank, collecting letters from START to END. They will spell the answer to this joke:

Knock, knock. Who's there? **Tank.** Tank who?

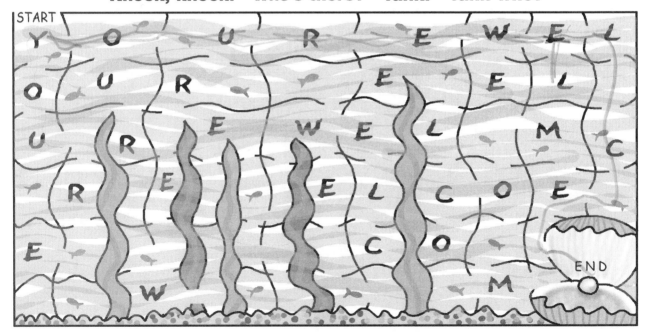

Knock knock!
Who's there?
Wendy.
Wendy who?
Wendy today, sunny tomorrow!

Knock knock!
Who's there?
Pencil.
Pencil who?
Pencil fall down if you
    don't buckle your belt!

Knock knock!
Who's there?
Boleyn.
Boleyn who?
Boleyn alley!

Knock knock!
Who's there?
Goat.
Goat who?
Goat to the door and answer it!

Knock knock!
Who's there?
Sadie.
Sadie who?
Sadie same thing over and over!

Knock knock!
Who's there?
Germany.
Germany who?
Germany people are coming over?

What am I?

I cannot be seen, and I cannot be felt. No one can hear me and I have no smell. I lie around stars, I fill empty holes, and I hide under hills.

What am I?

Darkness

Knock knock!
Who's there?
Waiter.
Waiter who?
Waiter minute!

Knock knock!
Who's there?
I-8.
I-8 who?
I-8 lunch at noon.
  When's dinner?

Knock knock!
Who's there?
Nan.
Nan who?
Nan that I know!

What's So Funny

Knock knock!
Who's there?
Max.
Max who?
Max-imum penalty
for the crime!

Knock knock!
Who's there?
Haydn.
Haydn who?
Haydn-go-seek is fun!

Knock knock!
Who's there?
Omar.
Omar who?
Omar goodness gracious!

Fun Fact

No Rhyme or Reason
Everybody loves a good rhyming song. Though it's easy to rhyme almost every word in the English language, there are exceptions. You'd be hard-pressed to find a word in the English language that rhymes with "orange," "silver," or "purple." ("Burple" doesn't count!)

Knock knock!
Who's there?
Sarah.
Sarah who?
'Sarah 'nother joke we can tell?

Knock knock!
Who's there?
Buster.
Buster who?
Bus-ter the park comes every hour!

Knock knock!
Who's there?
Thoreau.
Thoreau who?
Thoreau the ball!

Knock knock!
Who's there?
Hawaii.
Hawaii who?
I'm fine, Hawaii you?

It's Me!

Fill in the answers to the clues, one letter in each numbered space. Then transfer the letters to the boxes that have the same numbers. When all the boxes are filled in correctly, you will have the answer to this joke:

Knock, knock.

Who's there?

Shirley.

Shirley who?

A. O C N T M   Paper toys flown by strings.
   15 3 14 20 13

B. A L S K E D   Between spring and winter.
   1 12 19 11 6 4

C. ___ ___ ___   For what reason?
   25 2 8

D. ___ i ___ ___ ___   Covered in wool.
   18 9 17 5 22

E. ___ ___ ___ ___   A person, place, or thing.
   16 24 10 23

F. ___ ___   Close to, or beside.
   21 7

1 a	2 b	3 c	4 d	5 E	6 F	7 G		8 h	9 i	10 g		11	12	13	14

15	16	17	18		19	20		21	22		23	24	25	!

What am I?

As I grow up I grow down. I travel in groups but stay close to my family. I love to swim, but when the weather turns cold, I fly away. **What am I?**

A gosling (baby goose)

Knock knock!
Who's there?
Ozzie.
Ozzie who?
Oz-zie you later!

Knock knock!
Who's there?
Ireland.
Ireland who?
Ire-land you some money for lunch!

Knock knock!
Who's there?
Thistle.
Thistle who?
Thistle be the last time I tell you!

Knock knock!
Who's there?
Bertha.
Bertha who?
My Bertha-day's just around the corner!

Knock knock!
Who's there?
Gwen.
Gwen who?
Gwen will I see you again?

Knock knock!
Who's there?
Tank.
Tank who?
Tank goodness you answered the door!

Knock knock!
Who's there?
Fish.
Fish who?
Fish-us temper will get you nowhere!

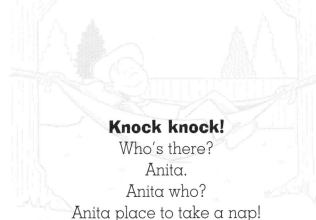

Knock knock!
Who's there?
Anita.
Anita who?
Anita place to take a nap!

Knock knock!
Who's there?
Soup.
Soup who?
Soup-erman has special powers!

Knock knock!
Who's there?
Handel.
Handel who?
Handel with care!

Knock knock!
Who's there?
Abby.
Abby who?
Abby days are here again!

Try This

Soap Suds Fun
Standing over the bathroom sink, rub a little bit of liquid soap between your hands. Wet your hands with just a drop of water. Then, keeping the tips of your fingers and palms together, slowly open the middle of your hands to form a tunnel. Gently blow through the tunnel in your hands, and huge bubbles should appear like magic.

Knock knock!
Who's there?
Blue.
Blue who?
Blue your nose!

Knock knock!
Who's there?
Fido.
Fido who?
Fido I have to do everything?

37

Knock knock!
Who's there?
Distress.
Distress who?
Distress is the one I wore to the party!

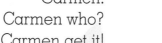

Knock knock!
Who's there?
Meow.
Meow who?
Take meow to the ball game!

Knock knock!
Who's there?
Carmen.
Carmen who?
Carmen get it!

Knock knock!
Who's there?
Xavier.
Xavier who?
Xavier breath!

Knock knock!
Who's there?
Grimm.
Grimm who?
Grimm and bear it!

Knock knock!
Who's there?
Taipei.
Taipei who?
Tai-pei letter and mail it!

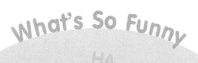

Knock knock!
Who's there?
Washer.
Washer who?
Washer don't know
won't hurt you!

Knock knock!
Who's there?
Jimmy.
Jimmy who?
Jimmy your money, this is a stickup!

Chapter 4
Knock-Knock Your Socks Off

Knock knock!
Who's there?
Reuben.
Reuben who?
Reuben my eyes, I'm sleepy!

Knock knock!
Who's there?
Sausage.
Sausage who?
Sausage nice things in the shop!

Knock knock!
Who's there?
Rosina.
Rosina who?
Rosina garden is lovely!

Knock knock!
Who's there?
Kipper.
Kipper who?
Kipper your eyes open for the signs!

Knock knock!
Who's there?
Pudding.
Pudding who?
Pudding your shoes on before your pants is a silly idea!

Knock knock!
Who's there?
Weed.
Weed who?
Weed better mow the lawn!

What am I?

I've got two really big front teeth that help me cut right through shrubs and even trees. I am known for building dams. These dams help slow down water and make deep pools where I love to splash around. **What am I?**

A beaver

Knock knock!
Who's there?
Nose.
Nose who?
Nose a lot of people!

Knock knock!
Who's there?
Rufus.
Rufus who?
Rufus on fire!

Knock knock!
Who's there?
Fletcher.
Fletcher who?
Fletcher feet do the walking!

Knock knock!
Who's there?
Stan.
Stan who?
Stan back, I'm coming through!

Try This

Magnet Magic
Did you know that a powerful magnet can work through paper, cardboard, and even water? Impress your friends with this trick. Put a paper clip in a glass that's mostly filled with water. Tell your friends you can get the paper clip out of the water without getting wet. Then slide the magnet along the glass until it connects with the paper clip. Move the magnet and the paper clip up the glass and above the surface of the water, until you can reach in and grab the paper clip without getting your fingers wet.

Knock knock!
Who's there?
F-2.
F-2 who?
F-2 go to the bathroom!

Knock knock!
Who's there?
Passion.
Passion who?
Just passion through!

Which Window?

Laura is visiting a friend who lives in an old apartment building. Use the clues to find out who will answer the door when Laura knock knocks!

- Laura's friend is not using the computer.
- The kid to the left of Laura's friend has a pet.
- Laura's friend does not know how to knit.
- Laura's friend has a window with curtains.

EXTRA FUN: Read the letters in the windows from bottom to top, and right to left. You will find the answer to this joke:

Knock, knock.
Who's there?
Juan.
Juan who?

Knock knock!
Who's there?
Warrior.
Warrior who?
Warrior been?

Knock knock!
Who's there?
Square.
Square who?
Square are we going?

Fun Fact

Sneaky Creatures
There are 84 different types of chameleons on the planet. They have special cells in their skin that allow them to blend in with their surroundings. This way, it is hard for enemies to find them. But watch out—if a chameleon gets angry, it can turn bright red.

Knock knock!
Who's there?
Sincerely.
Sincerely who?
Sincerely, we still have time for breakfast!

Knock knock!
Who's there?
Diane.
Diane who?
Diane to get in the door!

Knock knock!
Who's there?
Yoda.
Yoda who?
Yoda greatest, baby!

Knock knock!
Who's there?
Oakham.
Oakham who?
Oakham all ye faithful!

Knock knock!
Who's there?
Goshen.
Goshen who?
Goshen's great for swimming!

Knock knock!
Who's there?
Eight ball.
Eight ball who?
Eight ball the food!

Knock knock!
Who's there?
Kismet.
Kismet before anyone sees us!

Knock knock!
Who's there?
Rick.
Rick who?
Rick-ety bridge fell down!

Knock knock!
Who's there?
Sultan.
Sultan who?
Sultan pepper shakers!

Knock knock!
Who's there?
Cockadoodle.
Cockadoodle who?
Cockadoodle doo, not cockadoodle who!

Knock knock!
Who's there?
Mica.
Mica who?
Mi-ca is in the shop!

Knock knock!
Who's there?
Atch.
Atch who?
Bless you!

Comic relief:

Words to Know

A funny moment in a play or show that breaks up a very serious scene. Comic relief comes just in the nick of time when everything seems to be very tense and just too serious.

Knock knock!
Who's there?
Letter.
Letter who?
Letter ask us all she wants!

Knock knock!
Who's there?
Bjorn.
Bjorn who?
Bjorn to run!

Knock knock!
Who's there?
Maude.
Maude who?
Maude in the U.S.A.!

Knock knock!
Who's there?
Comet.
Comet who?
Com-et a crime and you'll go to jail!

Knock knock!
Who's there?
Quebec.
Quebec who?
Quebec to the beginning!

Knock knock!
Who's there?
Insect.
Insect who?
Insect your name here!

Knock knock!
Who's there?
Amish.
Amish who?
Amish you, do you miss me?

Knock knock!
Who's there?
Ooze.
Ooze who?
Ooze in charge around here?

Knock knock!
Who's there?
Fajita.
Fajita who?
'Fajita 'nother thing, I'll be sick!

Knock knock!
Who's there?
Wilma.
Wilma who?
Wilma headache ever go away?

Knock knock!
Who's there?
Minerva.
Minerva who?
Minerva-s wreck!

Knock knock!
Who's there?
Honeycomb.
Honeycomb who?
Honeycomb your
    hair, it's a mess!

What am I?

Hiya there mate! I carry my young in a pouch and I call him Joey. I hop around Australia and I'm cute as can be.
What am I?

A kangaroo

Knock knock!
Who's there?
Dennis.
Dennis who?
Dennis is going to fix my toothache!

Knock knock!
Who's there?
Worm.
Worm who?
Worm yourself by the fireplace!

Knock knock!
Who's there?
Amir.
Amir who?
Amir so let me in!

Knock knock!
Who's there?
Les.
Les who?
Les go home!

What's So Funny

HA HA HA HA HA HA

Knock knock!
Who's there?
Isadore.
Isadore who?
Isadore open?

Knock knock!
Who's there?
Ford.
Ford who?
Ford he's a jolly good fellow!

Half a Chance

This young lady only got half of her picture printed! Complete her portrait by copying the first half, square by square, into the empty grid.

Next, figure out which letter goes into each box, below. When you are finished, you will learn the second half of her name, too!

Knock, knock.
Who's there?
Alison.
Alison who?

E-4	Q-5	E+4	T-1	M+2	14
A	L	I	S	O	N

T+3	T-5	M+1	A+3	-5	V-4	12	D-3	J+4	G-3
W	O	N	D	E	R	L	A	O	d

47

Shhhhhhh!

Knock knock!
Who's there?
Butter.
Butter who?
Butter if I keep it a secret!

Knock knock!
Who's there?
Dummy.
Dummy who?
Dummy a favor and be quiet!

Knock knock!
Who's there?
Tamara.
Tamara who?
Tamara is Thursday!

Knock knock!
Who's there?
Handsome.
Handsome who?
Handsome chips to me, I'm hungry!

Knock knock!
Who's there?
Luke.
Luke who?
Luke out, I'm going to tell another knock-knock joke!

Knock knock!
Who's there?
Throat.
Throat who?
Throat out if it's rotten!

Knock knock!
Who's there?
Blue.
Blue who?
Blue away in the wind!

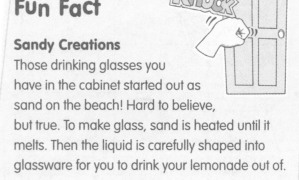

Fun Fact

Sandy Creations
Those drinking glasses you have in the cabinet started out as sand on the beach! Hard to believe, but true. To make glass, sand is heated until it melts. Then the liquid is carefully shaped into glassware for you to drink your lemonade out of.

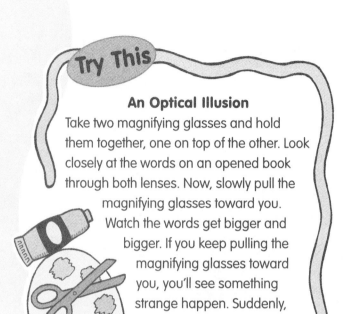

Try This

An Optical Illusion

Take two magnifying glasses and hold them together, one on top of the other. Look closely at the words on an opened book through both lenses. Now, slowly pull the magnifying glasses toward you. Watch the words get bigger and bigger. If you keep pulling the magnifying glasses toward you, you'll see something strange happen. Suddenly, the words flip. This is because the lenses bent the light rays!

Knock knock!
Who's there?
Quill.
Quill who?
Quill you marry me?

Knock knock!
Who's there?
Fanny.
Fanny who?
Fanny body home?

Knock knock!
Who's there?
Needle.
Needle who?
Needle little love in your life?

Knock knock!
Who's there?
Tom.
Tom who?
Tomcat ate your tongue?

Knock knock!
Who's there?
Woody.
Woody who?
Woody want from me?

Knock knock!
Who's there?
Jeannette.
Jeannette who?
'Jeann-ette has a lot of holes in it!

Knock knock!
Who's there?
Harmony.
Harmony who?
Harmony more knock knocks do you
    want to hear?

Knock knock!
Who's there?
Dexter.
Dexter who?
Dexter halls with boughs of holly!

Knock knock!
Who's there?
Faith.
Faith who?
Faith the music!

Try This

A Bugalicious Snack
Like insects? This snack is fun to make
and even more fun to eat. You'll
need some celery, peanut
butter, and raisins. Put some
peanut butter on the celery
sticks, then place the
raisins in the peanut butter.
You now have ants on a
log! Yummy!

Knock knock!
Who's there?
Al.
Al who?
Al be leaving soon!

Knock knock!
Who's there?
Thatcher.
Thatcher who?
Thatcher idea of a knock-knock joke?

Words to Know

shtick:
A show-business word that
means a comedian's routine. Most
comedians have a certain type of
act that they do much of the time.
Comedians go on tour to do
their shtick.

Knock knock!
Who's there?
Israeli.
Israeli who?
Israeli nice of you to come over!

Rhyme Time

Can you use eight single-syllable words that rhyme with "knock" to describe the actions and things in this picture?

EXTRA FUN: Can you see two other things that can be described using two-syllable words that end in "-ock"?

clock

block

What's So Funny

Knock knock!
Who's there?
Kent.
Kent who?
Kent you tell?

Knock knock!
Who's there?
Violet.
Violet who?
Violet a good meal go to waste?

Knock knock!
Who's there?
Spider.
Spider who?
'Spider everything, I'm still here!

Knock knock!
Who's there?
Elaine.
Elaine who?
Elaine on the highway is closed!

Knock knock!
Who's there?
Goose.
Goose who?
You goose who! I already know!

Knock knock!
Who's there?
Hewlett.
Hewlett who?
Hewlett you in the house?

Fun Fact

It's Electric!
Humans aren't the only ones who know how to communicate with each other. Many animals have a way of communicating. Birds chirp, dogs bark, and cats meow. There are some fish out there that have a very interesting way of letting other sea creatures know what's on their minds. About 500 different species of fish use electricity to communicate. A banded knife fish, for example, may scare off an enemy by flashing on and off!

Chapter 5
Who's That Knockin'?

Knock knock!
Who's there?
Paris.
Paris who?
Paris the thought!

Knock knock!
Who's there?
Eden.
Eden who?
Eden all the pudding!

Knock knock!
Who's there?
Homer.
Homer who?
Homer-run is great if
   you can hit one!

Knock knock!
Who's there?
Cash.
Cash who?
Cash whos are yummy!

Knock knock!
Who's there?
Plato.
Plato who?
Plato mashed potatoes!

Knock knock!
Who's there?
Ray.
Ray who?
Ray-ning all week long!

punch line:

Words to Know

A punch line has nothing to do with anyone punching. It is actually the funniest—or punchiest—part of a joke. Usually the punch line comes at the end of the joke. Ever listen to a long joke only to find out that the punch line wasn't so funny after all? That's no fun!

Knock knock!
Who's there?
Turner.
Turner who?
Turner 'round, quick!

crazy criss-cross

Unscramble each word and fit it into the numbered criss-cross grid.
When you are done, read down the shaded column to find the answer to this joke:

Knock, knock. **Who's there?** **Howie.** **Howie who?**

1. DEGEDLIHT
2. RRMEY
3. ENFI
4. ECXEITD
5. LRDOWNEFU
6. YREPK
7. UECHERFL
8. MSEAWOE
9. EWSLL
10. IAAFNTSTC
11. TRGEA
12. NLEEXCLET
13. PAHPY
14. DOGO
15. YUSNN

1. DELIGHTED
2. MERRY
3. FINE
4. EXCITED
5. D — L
6. E K
7. CHEERFUL
8. W E
9. SWELL
10. FANTASTIC
11. GREAT
12. EXCELLENT
13. HAPPY
14. GOOD
15. SUNNY

55

Knock knock!
Who's there?
Can't.
Can't who?
Can't elope!

Knock knock!
Who's there?
Noah.
Noah who?
Noah place to go!

Knock knock!
Who's there?
Warren.
Warren who?
Warren earth are you going?

Knock knock!
Who's there?
Salome.
Salome who?
Salome on a sandwich!

Knock knock!
Who's there?
Franz.
Franz who?
Franz, Romans, Countrymen!

Knock knock!
Who's there?
Wanda.
Wanda who?
Wanda off and you could get lost!

Knock knock!
Who's there?
Detour.
Detour who?
De-tour will take us to Spain!

What am I?

I collect acorns and bury them for cold weather. The problem is, I always forget where I've left them. Sometimes the acorns stay where I left them and grow into trees. I may be gray or black and I've got a bushy tail that makes me irresistible. **What am I?**

A squirrel

Knock knock!
Who's there?
Sandy.
Sandy who?
Sandy letter to your friend!

Knock knock!
Who's there?
Ina.
Ina who?
Ina few minutes I'm going to tell you
    another joke!

Knock knock!
Who's there?
Viper.
Viper who?
Viper your face, it's dirty!

Knock knock!
Who's there?
Canoe.
Canoe who?
Canoe come over
    for dinner?

Fun Fact

Keeping Warm
Ever wonder why certain
flowers close up at night? They do
this to stay warm. New seeds come
from the inside of the flower. It's important that
these seeds are protected in spring when
nighttime can still be a bit frosty.

Knock knock!
Who's there?
Zaire.
Zaire who?
Zaire it goes!

Knock knock!
Who's there?
Munich.
Munich who?
Munich me happy!

Knock knock!
Who's there?
Grub.
Grub who?
Grub on and hold tight!

What's So Funny

Knock knock!
Who's there?
Bette.
Bette who?
Bette your money
I'm right!

Knock knock!
Who's there?
Philip.
Philip who?
Philip the tub,
    I need a bath!

Knock knock!
Who's there?
Topic.
Topic who?
Topic a flower would be nice!

Knock once

Knock, knock.   Who's there?

Beth.   Beth who?

**Beth you can't
find the one time
the work KNOCK
is spelled
correctly!**   Beth you I can!

K	N	O	C	N	O	C	K
N	O	K	N	O	K	O	N
O	C	N	K	C	N	N	O
C	N	O	O	N	O	C	C
N	C	N	O	K	C	O	N
O	K	O	K	C	O	N	O
C	O	C	N	O	C	K	C
K	N	O	C	N	O	C	K

jest:

Not being serious. Sometimes a jest is a playful remark or a prank. In the Middle Ages, a jester was someone who worked at the king's court to entertain royalty.

Knock knock!
Who's there?
Hedda.
Hedda who?
Hedda 'nough, I'm leaving!

Knock knock!
Who's there?
Tail.
Tail who?
Tail everybody!

Knock knock!
Who's there?
Nun.
Nun who?
Nun of your business!

Try This

A Tasty Experiment
Cut up an apple into four parts and put the slices on a plate. Squeeze lemon juice over two of the four slices and let stand for three hours. When you come back, see what happened. The slices with lemon juice didn't turn brown, but the others did. That's because chemicals in the air turn the apple brown, but other chemicals in the lemon juice stop that from happening.

Knock knock!
Who's there?
Earl.
Earl who?
Earl you can ask for!

Knock knock!
Who's there?
Macon.
Macon who?
Macon a sandwich!

Knock knock!
Who's there?
Accordion.
Accordion who?
Accordion to the
   weatherman
   it's going to rain!

Knock knock!
Who's there?
Egypt.
Egypt who?
Egypt you when he sold you a
   broken watch!

Knock knock!
Who's there?
Henrietta.
Henrietta who?
Henrietta bad apple!

Knock knock!
Who's there?
Nantucket.
Nantucket who?
Nantucket but she said she'd give it back!

Knock knock!
Who's there?
Cecil.
Cecil who?
Cecil-ly jokes are fun!

Knock knock!
Who's there?
UC.
UC who?
UC what I see!

What am I?

You may cut me, but I'll grow back. I'm green when I get water and turn brown without it. People walk all over me and sometimes they play sports on me. **What am I?**

Grass

Knock knock!
Who's there?
Pea.
Pea who?
Pea U, something smells!

60

What's So Funny

Knock knock!
Who's there?
Rita.
Rita who?
Rita book!

Knock knock!
Who's there?
Van Gogh.
Van Gogh who?
Van Gogh and get me a cookie!

Knock knock!
Who's there?
Ants.
Ants who?
Ants in your pants!

Knock knock!
Who's there?
Reed.
Reed who?
Reed a newspaper!

Knock knock!
Who's there?
Cohen.
Cohen who?
Cohen around the merry-go-round.

Knock knock!
Who's there?
Venice.
Venice who?
Venice dinner going to be ready?

Knock knock!
Who's there?
Dots.
Dots who?
Dots not important!

Fun Fact

It's No Coincidence
Ever notice that some eggs are brown and others are white? Believe it or not, there are many different types of chickens out there. Brown eggs come from red hens and white eggs usually come from White Leghorn chickens. But most amazing is that there are even chickens that lay blue eggs, the Auracana chickens!

Knock knock!
Who's there?
Moe.
Moe who?
Moe cake, please!

Knock knock!
Who's there?
Isabel.
Isabel who?
Isabel needed on the door?

Knock knock!
Who's there?
Gopher.
Gopher who?
Gopher a long walk!

Knock knock!
Who's there?
CD.
CD who?
CD monkey in the cage!

Try This

In Motion
Take a piece of thin cardboard (for example, the side of a cereal box). Decorate it with a nature scene like a garden and a blue sky, or a seascape. Then make a little bird or a boat out of paper, something light that can move easily. Attach a paper clip to the bottom of your movable object. Put your object on the cardboard scene. Then get a magnet. You can move the small object around the cardboard by moving the magnet underneath the cardboard.

Knock knock!
Who's there?
Weasel.
Weasel who?
Weasel while you work!

Knock knock!
Who's there?
Guitar.
Guitar who?
Guitar coats before we go outside!

Who Is It?

Collect the letters as you find your way through the maze from START to END. As you read them in order, they will spell the answer to this joke:

Knock, knock.

Who's there?

Handsome.

Handsome who?

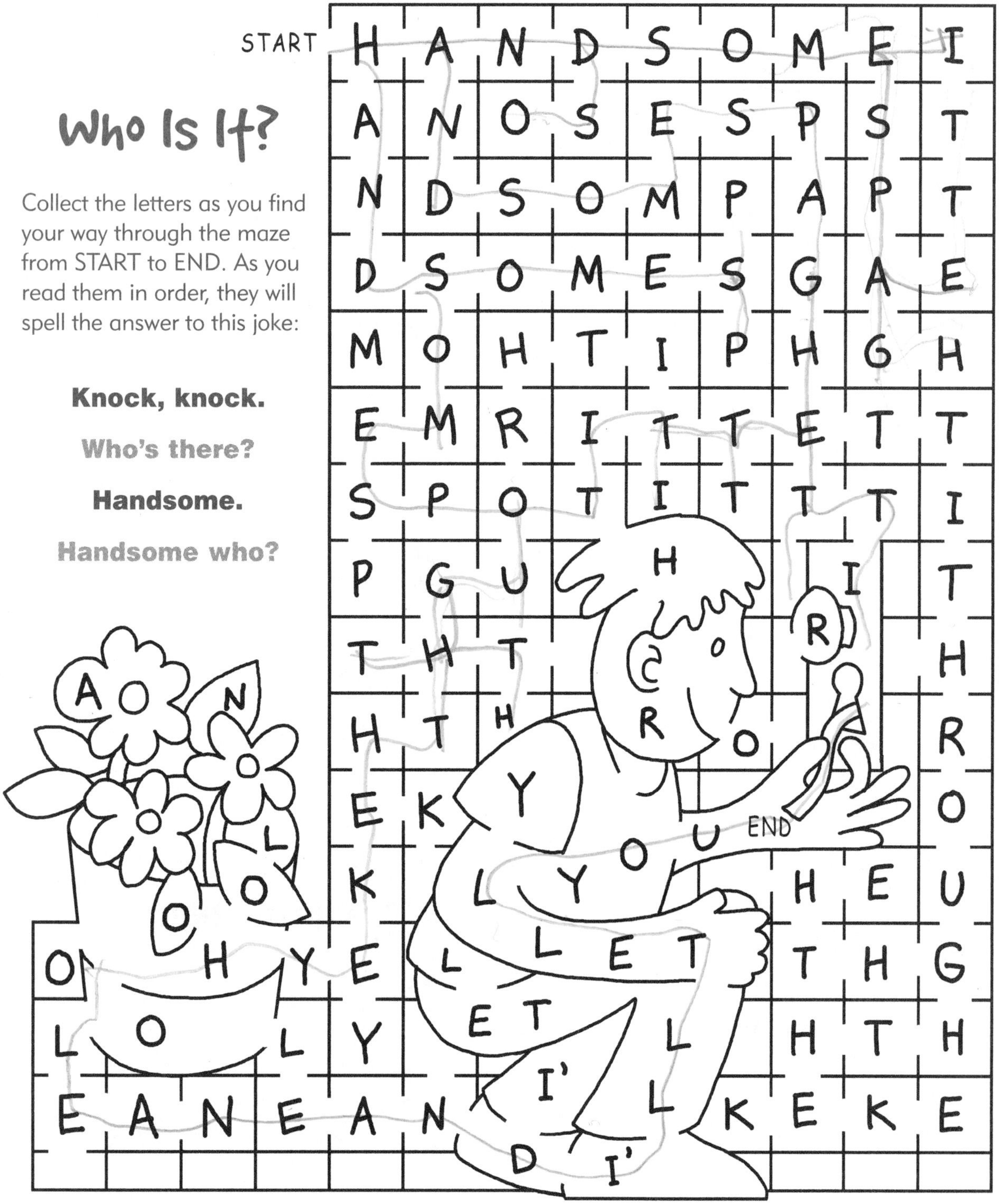

What's So Funny

Knock knock!
Who's there?
Blake.
Blake who?
Blake a leg!

Knock knock!
Who's there?
Olin.
Olin who?
Olin a day's work!

Knock knock!
Who's there?
Dana.
Dana who?
Dana talk with food in your mouth!

Knock knock!
Who's there?
One shoe.
One shoe who?
One shoe come over for a while?

Knock knock!
Who's there?
Alba.
Alba who?
Alba in the other room!

Knock knock!
Who's there?
Termites.
Termites who?
Termites the night!

Knock knock!
Who's there?
Mikey.
Mikey who?
Mikey won't work, can you open the door?

side-splitting:

Words to Know

Have you ever laughed so hard you thought you'd just bust? That's where the term "side-splitting" comes from. Side-splitting laughter is the type of laughter that takes over your whole body.

Chapter 6

One Two Three O'Clock Knock

Knock knock!
Who's there?
Trixie.
Trixie who?
There are Trixie can't do
because we didn't train him!

Knock knock!
Who's there?
Nobel.
Nobel who?
Nobel, that's why I knocked!

Knock knock!
Who's there?
Chris.
Chris who?
Chris-mas time is just around the
  corner!

Knock knock!
Who's there?
Orange.
Orange who?
Orange you happy?

Knock knock!
Who's there?
Amy.
Amy who?
Amy 'fraid I forgot the rest of the joke!

Knock knock!
Who's there?
Utica.
Utica who?
Utica long way!

What am I?

I am red with black dots, very small, and like to fly. I eat small tasty bugs and you usually find me resting comfortably on flowers in the summertime. People are always asking me to fly home. **What am I?**

A ladybug

Knock knock!
Who's there?
Soda.
Soda who?
Soda hole in your shirt!

Knock knock!
Who's there?
Tango.
Tango who?
Tango faster if you want!

Fun Fact

It's Like Armor
Do you know why there's so much skin on some kinds of fruit? Pineapples and other fruit have thick skins to keep out insects, protect from disease, and keep the fruit healthy and tasty for you to eat!

Knock knock!
Who's there?
Maida.
Maida who?
Maida world be at your fingertips!

Knock knock!
Who's there?
Wanda.
Wanda who?
Wanda bough breaks, the baby will fall!

Knock knock!
Who's there?
Juneau.
Juneau who?
Juneau what time it is?

Knock knock!
Who's there?
Doris.
Doris who?
Doris locked!

Knock knock!
Who's there?
Jamaica.
Jamaica who?
Jamaica mistake and no one ever forgets!

Mixed Up Endings

Collect all words with the same number above them and write them on the line with the corresponding number, below. Now, rearrange the words to get the answer for each joke!

3. Swiss	1. here!	4. over!	2. somebody	1. echo	3. like
1. There's	6. can	5. Australia!	4. minute	6. You	5. I'm
4. Anita	2. Pecan	1. a	6. yodel?	3. sound	2. time!
2. else	4. think	3. You	4. to	5. Yes,	4. it
3. clock!	1. in	5. from	2. next	1. terrible	3. a

---

1. Knock, knock. Who's there? **Who.** Who who?

---

2. Knock, knock. Who's there? **Pecan.** Pecan who?

---

3. Knock, knock. Who's there? **Cook.** Cook who?

---

4. Knock, knock. Who's there? **Anita.** Anita who?

---

5. Knock, knock. Who's there? **Kangar.** Kangar who?

---

6. Knock, knock. Who's there? **Little old lady.** Little old lady who?

Knock knock!
Who's there?
Dinosaur.
Dinosaur who?
Dinosaur because she fell down!

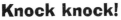

Knock knock!
Who's there?
Fossil.
Fossil who?
Fossil last time, let me in!

Knock knock!
Who's there?
Tennis.
Tennis who?
Ten is five plus five!

Knock knock!
Who's there?
Virtue.
Virtue who?
Virtue get that nice sweater?

Knock knock!
Who's there?
Wannetta.
Wannetta who?
Wannetta time, please!

Knock knock!
Who's there?
Brin.
Brin who?
Brin me some pie!

Words to Know

funny bone:

Ever hear someone say they are going to tickle your funny bone? Well, they aren't actually going to tickle a bone in your body. They mean they are going to make you laugh. Your funny bone is your sense of humor.

Knock knock!
Who's there?
Jack.
Jack who?
Jack your coat in the coatroom!

Knock knock!
Who's there?
Goose.
Goose who?
Goose see
   a doctor
   for that cough!

Knock knock!
Who's there?
Ben.
Ben who?
Ben waiting around for hours!

Knock knock!
Who's there?
Beryl.
Beryl who?
Beryl luck next time!

Knock knock!
Who's there?
Major.
Major who?
Major look!

Knock knock!
Who's there?
Wooden.
Wooden who?
Wooden you like to find out!

Knock knock!
Who's there?
Sam.
Sam who?
Sam person who told you the last
   knock-knock joke!

Knock knock!
Who's there?
Throne.
Throne who?
Throne out the garbage!

What's So Funny

Knock knock!
Who's there?
Gouda.
Gouda who?
Goudas can be!

Try This

The Power of Your Hair

Turn on the water in the bathroom sink so just a thin stream of water flows out. Then, comb your hair about twenty times. Put the comb near the water, but not touching it. Watch as the water bends to reach the comb. This is because of the static electricity in your hair!

Knock knock!
Who's there?
Beth.
Beth who?
Beth time of my life!

Knock knock!
Who's there?
Accord.
Accord who?
Accord of wood for the fireplace!

Wendy's Here

Knock, knock.

Who's there?

Wendy.

Wendy who?

Wendy boxes are all colored in, you will see who it is!

Color Code:
B - BROWN   G - GREEN
P - PEACH   R - RED
K - BLACK   L - LIGHT BLUE

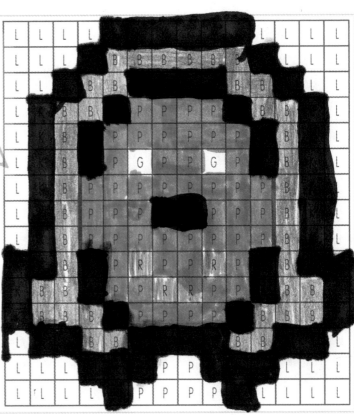

Knock knock!
Who's there?
Kentucky.
Kentucky who?
Kentucky you in at night!

Knock knock!
Who's there?
Colleen.
Colleen who?
Colleen up the kitchen
when you're done cookin'!

Knock knock!
Who's there?
Goddess.
Goddess who?
Goddess stop this madness!

Knock knock!
Who's there?
Evan.
Evan who?
Evan-ly angels!

Knock knock!
Who's there?
Howard
Howard who?
Howard I know?

Knock knock!
Who's there?
Kip.
Kip who?
Kip looking till we find it!

What am I?

I run over hills and around mountains. I jump rivers and make my way through thick forests. You can't go anywhere without me, and if you step outside your door, I'll be waiting there.
What am I?

The road

Knock knock!
Who's there?
Hello.
Hello who?
Hel-lo can you go?

Knock knock!
Who's there?
Swear.
Swear who?
Swear are we going?

Knock knock!
Who's there?
Ghana.
Ghana who?
Ghana go to town!

Knock knock!
Who's there?
Hyde.
Hyde who?
Hyde like to tell you another joke!

palindrome:

Words to Know

A word, sentence, or number that reads the same backward and forward. For example, the number 13531 is a palindrome. So is the name Bob.

Knock knock!
Who's there?
Faith.
Faith who?
Faith it, it's over!

Knock knock!
Who's there?
Vaughn.
Vaughn who?
Vaughn day we'll see each other again!

Knock knock!
Who's there?
Teacher.
Teacher who?
Teacher some manners!

Fun Fact

Down Deep
The deepest place on earth is located in the Pacific Ocean. It is called the Challenger Deep, and it's a very dark and cold place to be. The bottom of Challenger Deep is 35,813 feet below the surface of the water (that's almost 7 miles)! Hardly anything at all can live there!

Knock knock!
Who's there?
Buck.
Buck who?
Buck stops here!

Knock knock!
Who's there?
Dali.
Dali who?
Dali in the window sure is pretty!

Knock knock!
Who's there?
Lemmie.
Lemmie who?
Lemmie tell you a story!

Knock knock!
Who's there?
Foster.
Foster who?
Foster than a speeding bullet!

Knock knock!
Who's there?
Ogre.
Ogre who?
Ogre take a long walk!

Knock knock!
Who's there?
Tree.
Tree who?
Tree plus tree is six!

What's So Funny

Knock knock!
Who's there?
Wade.
Wade who?
Wade up, I've got more knock-knock jokes!

Knock knock!
Who's there?
Alaska.
Alaska who?
Alaska once more and that's it!

open the Door

Complete each of these seven knock-knock jokes by writing the name of one of the objects on this page into the blank spaces provided.

1. _____ your sister who I am!

2. _____ _____ like to know ?

3. _____ you come out and play?

4. _____ me! Who are you?

5. _____ you for for inviting me over!

6. _____ see you when you open the door!

7. _____ by you?

Knock knock!
Who's there?
Don't chew.
Don't chew who?
Don't chew know?

Knock knock!
Who's there?
Monroe.
Monroe who?
Monroe your boat!

absurd:

Words to Know

Completely ridiculous or silly. For example, it is absurd to think that there is a man living on the moon.

Knock knock!
Who's there?
Glitter.
Glitter who?
Glitter bug!

Knock knock!
Who's there?
Weirdo.
Weirdo you think you're going?

Try This

Make a Five-Headed Puppet
Spread your hand out on a piece of paper. Trace your hand and fingers onto the paper with a pencil. Glue some yarn on the tip of each finger tracing so it looks like hair. Then paste googly eyes on each of the five heads. Draw noses and mouths with crayons or colored pencils. Then cut out the whole hand tracing. Glue a Popsicle stick to the back of the paper hand and put on a puppet show.

Knock knock!
Who's there?
Island.
Island who?
Island on the house with my parachute!

Knock knock!
Who's there?
Adair.
Adair who?
'Ad-air once,
   but now I'm bald!

Knock knock!
Who's there?
Freeman.
Freeman who?
Free-man from his chains!

Knock knock!
Who's there?
Heaven.
Heaven who?
Heaven you heard enough knock-knock
   jokes?

Knock knock!
Who's there?
Pecan.
Pecan who?
Pecan somebody else!

Knock knock!
Who's there?
Band.
Band who?
Band from going there!

Knock knock!
Who's there?
Candace.
Candace who?
Candace be true?

Knock knock!
Who's there?
Habit.
Habit who?
Habit your way, I'll have it mine!

What am I?

I look like a fish and I live in water. But I'm not really a fish. I'm a mammal. I'm incredibly smart and I always have a smile on my face. Sometimes you'll see me doing tricks at the aquarium. **What am I?**

A dolphin

Try This

Taste Tests

Have you ever noticed that when you have a cold, you have less of an appetite? This is partly because we need our sense of smell to enjoy our food. With the help of a grownup, cut up a bunch of different vegetables, fruits, and cheeses with similar textures. One of you can be the taster, and the other will be the server. The server tells the taster to close his eyes and hold his nose. Then the server places a piece of food in the taster's mouth. The taster has to guess what the food is without using his sense of sight or smell. How easy do you think it will be to guess what you're eating?

Knock knock!
Who's there?
Fran.
Fran who?
Fran of mine is coming to town!

Knock knock!
Who's there?
Unit.
Unit who?
Unit me a sweater!

Knock knock!
Who's there?
Hugh.
Hugh who?
Hugh must have been a star!

Knock knock!
Who's there?
Klaus.
Klaus who?
Klaus the window!

Knock knock!
Who's there?
Amoeba.
Amoeba who?
Amoeba wrong, but I may be right!

Knock knock!
Who's there?
Chicken.
Chicken who?
Chicken to see if you're okay!

Knock knock!
Who's there?
Renata.
Renata who?
Renata jokes, I'll have
to learn some more!

Knock knock!
Who's there?
Mia.
Mia who?
Mia pants are on fire!

Knock knock!
Who's there?
Chess.
Chess who?
Chess the way it is!

Knock knock!
Who's there?
Yuri.
Yuri who?
Yuri great pal!

come and Get It!

Your mom is cooking dinner when, suddenly . . .

Knock, knock.

Who's there?

Gus.

Gus who?

To find the end of this mystery, start at the letter marked with a dot. As you spiral into the center, collect every other letter. Write them in order on the lines. When you reach the middle, head back out again, collecting all the letters that you skipped over the first time.

GUS
WHO'S
COMING
TO
DINNER!

Knock knock!
Who's there?
Pasta.
Pasta who?
Pasta potatoes please!

Knock knock!
Who's there?
Pasture.
Pasture who?
Pasture bedtime!

Knock knock!
Who's there?
Stu.
Stu who?
Stu you want to tell me something?

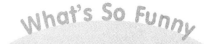

Knock knock!
Who's there?
May.
May who?
Mayday Mayday!

Knock knock!
Who's there?
Dwight.
Dwight who?
Dwight way is the best way!

Knock knock!
Who's there?
Colin.
Colin who?
Colin all kids!

Knock knock!
Who's there?
Alpaca.
Alpaca who?
Alpaca the suitcase before we go!

Fun Fact

Hot and Cold
The Sahara Desert is the largest desert in the world. It gets so hot there during the day, it is almost impossible to go more than four hours without water. At night, though, it can get so cold, the temperature may drop below freezing!

Words to Know

skit:

A short and funny play. A class might write a skit for a school performance. Sometimes a show will be made up of a few different skits.

Knock knock!
Who's there?
Sweden.
Sweden who?
Sweden sour chicken!

Knock knock!
Who's there?
Hammond.
Hammond who?
Hammond eggs make a good breakfast!

Knock knock!
Who's there?
Canoe.
Canoe who?
Canoe tell
    me a story?

Knock knock!
Who's there?
Lana.
Lana who?
Lana the free, home of the brave!

Knock knock!
Who's there?
Nanny.
Nanny who?
Nanny one home?

Knock knock!
Who's there?
Waddle.
Waddle who?
Waddle you give me for my birthday?

Fun Fact

Arachno-What?
Arachnophobia is the fear of spiders, but most of these creatures are nothing to be afraid of! Spiders are actually good to have around. Almost all of them are completely harmless, and they catch and eat pesky insects.

We Deliver!

It's fun to order takeout food and have it delivered. But it's even more fun if the delivery person has a yummy name! Choose from the middle initials and last names scattered down the right side of this page. Write them on the correct lines to create seven deliciously different delivery people who might come knock-knocking at your door to bring dinner!

1. Knock, knock. Who's there? Manilla. Manilla who?
   Manilla _____

2. Knock, knock. Who's there? Barbie. Barbie who?
   Barbie _____

3. Knock, knock. Who's there? Frank. Frank who?
   Frank _____

4. Knock, knock. Who's there? Hamen. Hamen who?
   Hamen _____

5. Knock, knock. Who's there? Roland. Roland who?
   Roland _____

6. Knock, knock. Who's there? Marsha. Marsha who?
   Marsha _____

7. Knock, knock. Who's there? Sultan. Sultan who?
   Sultan _____

N.

Pepper

Mallow

Butter

Scream

Q.

Beans

Chicken

I.   Eggs

Knock knock!
Who's there?
Lionel.
Lionel who?
Lionel get you nowhere!

Knock knock!
Who's there?
Rich.
Rich who?
Rich man is a poor man with money!

Knock knock!
Who's there?
Orson.
Orson who?
'Orson carriage!

Knock knock!
Who's there?
Dishes.
Dishes who?
Dishes the police,
   open the door!

Knock knock!
Who's there?
Spider.
Spider who?
I spider hiding in the yard!

Knock knock!
Who's there?
Aspen.
Aspen who?
A-spen around until I get dizzy!

Knock knock!
Who's there?
Holly.
Holly who?
Holly days are fun!

What am I?

I'm fast as can be, and built for speed. I've got huge claws, and my nest is grand. I live in high cliffs, in canyon walls, and even on city skyscrapers.
What am I?

A falcon

84

Knock knock!
Who's there?
Pest.
Pest who?
Pest wishes to you!

Knock knock!
Who's there?
April.
April who?
April showers bring May flowers!

Knock knock!
Who's there?
Bach.
Bach who?
Bach to the future!

What's So Funny

Knock knock!
Who's there?
Ivan.
Ivan who?
Ivan extra few minutes
for some more jokes!

Knock knock!
Who's there?
Heart.
Heart who?
Heart it through the grapevine!

Knock knock!
Who's there?
Telly.
Telly who?
Telly your brother to come home!

Knock knock!
Who's there?
Raisin.
Raisin who?
Raisin our hands
before we speak!

Try This

Make a Rainbow
On a sunny day, get the garden hose and then stand with your back to the sun. Adjust the hose nozzle so it just lightly mists water. Hold the hose up in front of you, and then look closely. You will see a rainbow in the mist.

funny friends

We've hidden the first half of fifteen knock-knock names in the grid. Look carefully as you highlight each name, and you'll find each person's last name, too. One is done for you!

HINT: Middle initials are sometimes included.

EXTRA FUN: Turn each name into a knock-knock joke!

~~LUKE~~	ELLA	ALBIE	TOM	TIM
PAT	M. GLADYS	BABE	MATT	WANDA
IMA	HANK	MAURA	LEWIS	ABBY

```
W A N D A B. F R E N Z S M.
M B A L B I E C. I N G U G
A B O B. S O M S R A S L L
U I T O M A. T O W E T U A
R R U B M I T O T B M K D
A R M E K A C E. T A P E Y
L M O S V M S M Z M Z O S
E E H A N K R. C H I F U F
S L L R A B R A B S O T R
S L T B A B E E. F A C E I
E S S U R T T A M S O D
M K R A L C N. S I W E L A
A B B Y B I R T H D A Y Y
```

parody:

Words to Know

A play, sometimes a musical, that is meant to be very funny and often makes fun of something.

Knock knock!
Who's there?
Summer.
Summer who?
Summer time and the living is good!

Knock knock!
Who's there?
Quiche.
Quiche who?
Quiche me, I love you!

Knock knock!
Who's there?
Hiram.
Hiram who?
Hiram your best friend, don't you
remember me?

Knock knock!
Who's there?
Hacienda.
Hacienda who?
Hacienda the story!

Knock knock!
Who's there?
Whoville.
Whoville who?
Whoville answer the door ven I knock?

Knock knock!
Who's there?
Dale.
Dale who?
Dale come if you invite them!

Knock knock!
Who's there?
Root.
Root who?
Root for me at the game!

87

Knock knock!
Who's there?
Phyllis.
Phyllis who?
Phyllis in on the details!

Knock knock!
Who's there?
Meter.
Meter who?
Meter in the lobby!

guffaw:

A loud burst of uncontrollable laughter. If you're watching a movie that has many funny things happening, you might not be able to control your laughter. That's when you are likely to guffaw!

Words to Know

Knock knock!
Who's there?
Carrie.
Carrie who?
Carrie me home, I'm tired!

Try This

Learn to See Around Corners!
Find a ruler, some tape, and a small mirror. Carefully tape the mirror to the ruler, making sure not to cover up the mirror with the tape. Stand to one side of a door and hold the ruler outside the doorway, so that the mirror is at the farther end. If you move the mirror around, you will be able to see different things in the room through the mirror!

Knock knock!
Who's there?
Rhoda.
Rhoda who?
Rhoda donkey at the zoo!

Knock knock!
Who's there?
Rozette.
Rozette who?
Rozette a bug, now she feels sick!

Chapter 8

Knock-Knock Yourself Silly

Knock knock!
Who's there?
Olive.
Olive who?
Olive you too!

Knock knock!
Who's there?
Lima bean.
Lima bean who?
Lima bean working on the railroad!

Knock knock!
Who's there?
Dee.
Dee who?
Dee-licious!

Knock knock!
Who's there?
Lisbon.
Lisbon who?
Lisbon to the movies twice this week!

Knock knock!
Who's there?
Cher.
Cher who?
Cher would be nice to see you again!

Knock knock!
Who's there?
Hive.
Hive who?
Hive got my eye on you!

Knock knock!
Who's there?
Stuart.
Stuart who?
Stuart up and serve it while it's hot!

Fun Fact

Penguin Pairs
Male and female penguins have a very interesting way of courting each other. If a male penguin is interested in a female penguin, he may offer her small pebbles as a gift. If she accepts, he knows he has won her heart.

What am I?

I can be found in marshes, swamps, lakes, and ponds. I am famous in the South. I can grow up to 13 feet long, and as an adult I may weigh up to 500 pounds. I catch my food by clamping my jaws shut over them. **What am I?**

An alligator

Knock knock!
Who's there?
Anita.
Anita who?
Anita good rest!

Knock knock!
Who's there?
Tonto.
Tonto who?
Tonto get ready for school!

Knock knock!
Who's there?
Isaac.
Isaac who?
Isaac-ly who you think it is!

Knock knock!
Who's there?
Chair.
Chair who?
Chair your secrets with me!

Knock knock!
Who's there?
Vine.
Vine who?
Vine-derful news!

Knock knock!
Who's there?
Cedar.
Cedar who?
Cedar plane flying in the air!

Knock knock!
Who's there?
Roxanne.
Roxanne who?
Roxanne sand are at the beach!

Ho, Ho, Ho

The answer to this joke is missing the letters a, e, i, o, and u. Can you fit them in the proper blanks?

_h, y__ b_t_ w_tch __t,
y__ b_t_ n_t cry,
y__ b_t_ n_t p__t,
_'m t_ll_ng y__ why —
S_nt_ Cl__s _s c_m_ng
t_ t_wn!

Knock knock!
Who's there?
Grant.
Grant who?
Grant me a wish!

Knock knock!
Who's there?
Babbit.
Babbit who?
Babbit in the garden
   ate our lettuce!

Knock knock!
Who's there?
Luke.
Luke who?
Luke through the
   peephole and
   you'll see!

Knock knock!
Who's there?
Sole.
Sole who?
'Sole new day!

Knock knock!
Who's there?
Iguana.
Iguana who?
Iguana tell you something!

Knock knock!
Who's there?
Diploma.
Diploma who?
Diploma is coming to fix the pipes!

Try This

Yesterday and Today

Collect some old photos of grandparents
or other older relatives. Now get some
pictures of you and your friends.
Put the new photos next to the old
photos to see how different
things are today. What kind
of clothes did the people in
the old photos wear? Are
there other differences you
can detect?

Knock knock!
Who's there?
Chelsea.
Chelsea who?
Chel-sea you later!

Knock knock!
Who's there?
Fruit.
Fruit who?
Fruit of all evil!

Knock knock!
Who's there?
Utah.
Utah who?
Utah-king to me?

Knock knock!
Who's there?
Sabina.
Sabina who?
Sabina long time since I told you a
    knock-knock joke!

Knock knock!
Who's there?
Bolivia.
Bolivia who?
Bolivia me, I know what I'm talking
    about!

Knock knock!
Who's there?
Watson.
Watson who?
Wats-on the radio?

Knock knock!
Who's there?
Latin.
Latin who?
Latin me through the door is a
    good idea!

Knock knock!
Who's there?
Peace.
Peace who?
Peace and carrots!

Knock knock!
Who's there?
Ike.
Ike who?
Ike could dance all night!

Knock knock!
Who's there?
Chicken.
Chicken who?
Chicken' out the situation!

vaudeville:

Words to Know

A staged performance including a lot of different types of acts. There could be singing, dancing, comedy, acrobats, and even animal tricks. Everyone loves a good vaudeville show!

Aye, Aye, Captain

First, figure out what word each letter and picture puzzle represents. Then, number the words in the proper order to create the answer to this joke:

Knock, knock.

Who's there?

Fire engine.

Fire engine who?

Fun Fact

Yawning for Air

Yawning when you're tired is actually a wake-up call for the brain. Your brain needs lots of oxygen, which is carried in your bloodstream to all parts of your body. When you're tired, your heart pumps more slowly. This means oxygen gets to your brain slowly. When you yawn, your brain gets the oxygen a lot faster. That makes your brain happy!

Knock knock!
Who's there?
Ken.
Ken who?
Ken you tell me something new?

Knock knock!
Who's there?
Banana.
Banana who?
Banana split, so ice creamed!

Knock knock!
Who's there?
Galway.
Galway who?
Galway or else!

Knock knock!
Who's there?
U-8.
U-8 who?
U-8 my candy bar!

Knock knock!
Who's there?
Harry.
Harry who?
Harry-planes fly overhead!

Knock knock!
Who's there?
Eliza.
Eliza who?
Eliza when he doesn't want anyone to know the truth!

What am I?

I can eat a thousand flying insects in one night. My favorite place to live is very close to others like me. I can hang out upside down all day long. One of the best things about me is that I fly around at night and I don't need the light.
What am I?

A bat

Where in the World?

Use each of the place names from around the world to complete one of the jokes below. Be careful—there are more names than you need.
EXTRA FUN: Turn each of the place names into a knock-knock!

1. _____ questions, you give the answers!

2. _____ matter? Cat got your tongue?

3. _____ to the party!

4. _____ lots of wood with my chain saw!

5. _____ come out and play?

6. _____ me very happy!

7. _____ go home now!

8. _____ ride my bike?

9. _____ a puppy for Christmas!

10. _____ have it, I don't want it!

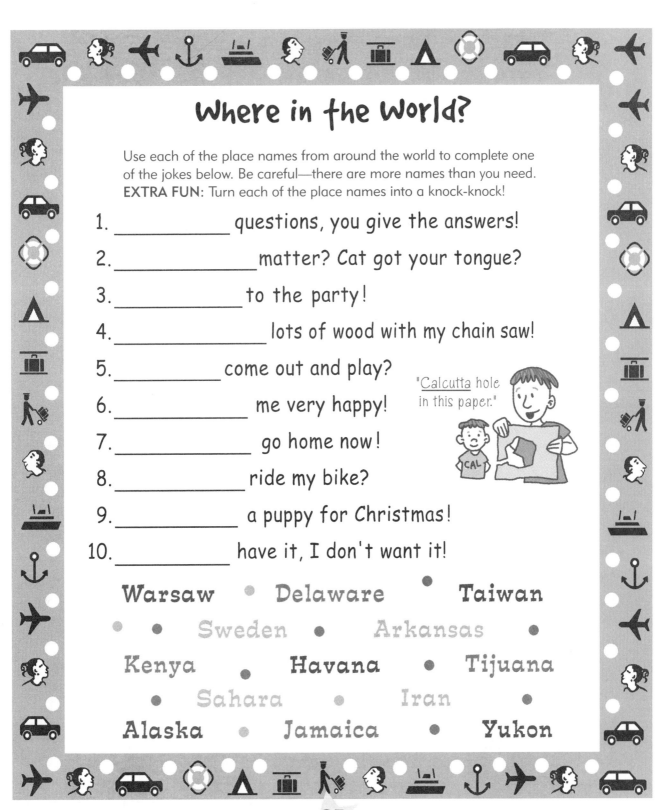

"Calcutta hole in this paper."

Warsaw • **Delaware** • **Taiwan**

Sweden • Arkansas

Kenya • **Havana** • **Tijuana**

Sahara • Iran

Alaska • **Jamaica** • **Yukon**

Knock knock!
Who's there?
Daryl.
Daryl who?
Daryl only be one chance!

Knock knock!
Who's there?
Tom.
Tom who?
Tom-ah-toes are yummy!

Try This

Make Your Own Rain Catcher
Tape a ruler to the inside of a coffee can or small jar. Then set the jar outside the next time it rains. After the rain ends, you can measure how many of inches of rain have fallen during the rainstorm!

Knock knock!
Who's there?
Barry.
Barry who?
Barry sorry for the mix-up!

Knock knock!
Who's there?
Guava.
Guava who?
Guava good time!

Knock knock!
Who's there?
Ada.
Ada who?
Ada lot of candy
    and now I have a
    tummy ache!

Knock knock!
Who's there?
Minotaur.
Minotaur who?
Minotaur ready, we'll go!

Knock knock!
Who's there?
Vera.
Vera who?
Vera you going for dinner?

Knock knock!
Who's there?
Czar.
Czar who?
Czar-y about spilling the drink!

Knock knock!
Who's there?
Randy.
Randy who?
Ran-dy track twice!

Knock knock!
Who's there?
Waddle.
Waddle who?
Waddle you give me?

spoof:
A light and playful way of making fun of something. You might see a television show, a movie, or a play that's a spoof, or even read a story that spoofs something or someone.

Words to Know

Knock knock!
Who's there?
Illegals.
Illegals who?
Ill-egals stay in the nest till they're old enough to fly!

Knock knock!
Who's there?
Fission.
Fission who?
Fission for trout!

What's So Funny

Knock knock!
Who's there?
Wheelbarrow.
Wheelbarrow who?
Wheel-barrow the car and go for a ride!

Knock knock!
Who's there?
Beehive.
Beehive who?
Beehive yourself or you'll get in trouble!

Knock knock!
Who's there?
Gwen.
Gwen who?
Gwen are we leaving?

Knock knock!
Who's there?
Thurston.
Thurston who?
Thurston for a milkshake!

What am I?

I travel in packs and have beautiful fur. I can survive almost anywhere as long as there is plenty to eat. My scientific name is *Canis lupus*, but you know me from a famous fairy tale. I was framed, I tell you! Little Red Riding Hood set me up!
What am I?

A wolf

Knock knock!
Who's there?
Honey.
Honey who?
Honey way home we'll stop for ice cream!

Knock knock!
Who's there?
Carl.
Carl who?
Carl get you there faster!

Knock knock!
Who's there?
Warner.
Warner who?
Warner lift to school?

What's So Funny

HA HA HA HA HA HA

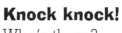

Knock knock!
Who's there?
China.
China who?
China tell you something!

Knock knock!
Who's there?
Farrah.
Farrah who?
Farrah 'nough!

Chapter 9
A Knock Here, a Knock There

Knock knock!
Who's there?
Egg.
Egg who?
Eggstremely cold!

Knock knock!
Who's there?
Andy.
Andy who?
He did it once, Andy did it again!

Knock knock!
Who's there?
Minnie.
Minnie who?
Minnie more miles to go!

Knock knock!
Who's there?
Eiffel.
Eiffel who?
Eiffel sick!

Knock knock!
Who's there?
Sybil.
Sybil who?
Sybil-ization!

Knock knock!
Who's there?
Curry.
Curry who?
Curry the package home!

Try This

Invent Your Own Animals

Look through some old magazines to see how many animal pictures you can find. Cut out the legs of a dog, the ears of a cat, the face of a chicken, the body of a giraffe, or whatever parts you want from the other animals that you see. Make your own combinations of the cutouts, and come up with as many "new" animals as you can. Then give them all funny names, like "dogachickiraffe"! Now make up a story about where these types of creature can be found, what they like to eat, and what strange habits they have!

gag:

Words to Know

A prank or joke that makes people laugh. Sometimes a comedian will have a running gag in the show (that means the same gag will be repeated over and over again). Running gags can also be part of television shows, movies, and plays.

Knock knock!
Who's there?
Newark.
Newark who?
Newark for you when you finish the old work!

Knock knock!
Who's there?
Aretha.
Aretha who?
Aretha flowers for the door!

Knock knock!
Who's there?
Gecko.
Gecko who?
Gecko-ing or you'll be late!

Knock knock!
Who's there?
Duke.
Duke who?
Duke you come here often?

Knock knock!
Who's there?
Gladys.
Gladys who?
Gladys lunch time, I'm starved!

Knock knock!
Who's there?
Ears.
Ears who?
Ears looking at you, kid!

Knock knock!
Who's there?
Grape.
Grape who?
Grape pie, can I have some more!

Knock knock!
Who's there?
Lacey.
Lacey who?
Lacey days of summer!

Knock knock!
Who's there?
Wafer.
Wafer who?
Wafer the bus!

Knock knock!
Who's there?
Enid.
Enid who?
Enid to take a nap!

Fun Fact

Freeze Frame
When you sneeze, all of your body functions stop—even your heart stops pumping for a moment. Whenever you sneeze, air rushes through your body at a rate of 100 miles per hour. And it's impossible to sneeze with your eyes open!

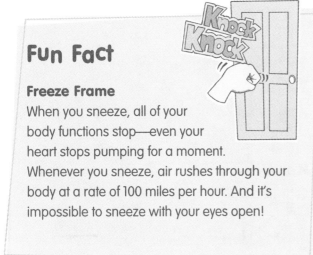

What am I?

I look like a star in the sky but I live at the bottom of the sea. I'm tough on the outside and I've got a great talent: If I lose an arm I can easily grow a new one back! **What am I?**

A starfish

Knock knock!
Who's there?
Carrie.
Carrie who?
Carrie these boxes, they're not heavy!

Knock knock!
Who's there?
Tommy.
Tommy who?
My Tommy hurts from too much pie!

Knock knock!
Who's there?
Doughnut.
Doughnut who?
Doughnut be scared, it's only a joke!

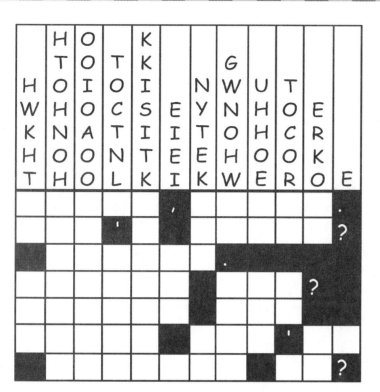

DO I KNOW YOU?

The letters in each column go in the squares directly below them, but not in the same order! Black squares are for punctuation, and the spaces between the words. When you have correctly filled in the grid, you will have a silly conversation between two people on opposite sides of a door!

Who's there?

Hey! Open the door!

Don't Forget to Brush

See if you can fit all the words into their proper place in the grid. When you are finished, read down the center column to get the answer to this joke:

Knock, knock.

Who's there?

Tuba.

Tuba who?

APE
IT'S
CAT
SHY
NET
DOG
CUT
ETC.
EBB
PAN
ATE
LOG
USE
STY

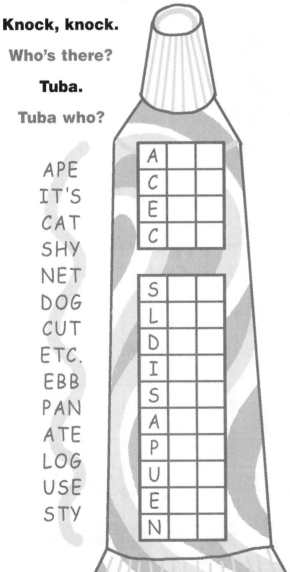

A		
C		
E		
C		

S		
L		
D		
I		
S		
A		
P		
U		
E		
N		

Knock knock!
Who's there?
Oscar.
Oscar who?
Oscar again, she didn't hear you the first time!

Knock knock!
Who's there?
Honeydew.
Honeydew who?
Honeydew-nuts are yummy!

Knock knock!
Who's there?
Congo.
Congo who?
Congo out, I'm grounded!

Knock knock!
Who's there?
Woodstock.
Woodstock who?
Woodstock up on food if I were you!

Knock knock!
Who's there?
Lorraine.
Lorraine who?
Lorraine is falling and I'm getting
    soaked!

Knock knock!
Who's there?
Daisy.
Daisy who?
Daisy goes to school, nights he sleeps!

Knock knock!
Who's there?
Bored.
Bored who?
Bored of education!

Try This

A Neighborhood Scrapbook
Go on a nature walk in your
neighborhood. See how many different
types of flowers and animals you can
    identify. When you get home, look
    for pictures of the flowers and
    animals in magazines. Cut out
        some of these. Then paste the
        pictures onto construction
        paper. Punch holes in the
        construction paper and tie
        the pages together with a
        ribbon.

Knock knock!
Who's there?
Fresno.
Fresno who?
Fresno fun when he's angry!

Knock knock!
Who's there?
Beezer.
Beezer who?
Beezer black
    and yellow!

107

Dots Funny

Knock, knock. Who's there? **Dots.** Dots who?

Color in all the squares with a dot in the upper right-hand corner . . .

. . . and unscramble the words.

NAD OYU OT

and Dan   you   To

NIFD UOT!

Find   out!

What am I?

I live in the forest and I make loud noises with my beak when I find a tree with lots of tasty bugs in it. You can't mistake my sound. You may know my uncle—he's a funny cartoon character named Woody. **What am I?**

A woodpecker

Knock knock!
Who's there?
Seville.
Seville who?
Seville you come to the dance?

Knock knock!
Who's there?
Topeka.
Topeka who?
Topeka apples you
    have to go to the orchard!

Knock knock!
Who's there?
Hominy.
Hominy who?
Hominy times do I have to tell you?

Knock knock!
Who's there?
Tarzan.
Tarzan who?
Tarzan stripes!

Knock knock!
Who's there?
Moose.
Moose who?
Moose have been a long night!

Knock knock!
Who's there?
Disk.
Disk who?
Disk is a holdup,
    put your hands in the air!

whimsical:

Light or funny. Many things are whimsical. For example, knock-knock jokes are pretty whimsical! Stage-acting with a lot of clowning around is pretty whimsical too.

Knock knock!
Who's there?
Malcolm.
Malcolm who?
Malcolm it took you so long to answer
    the door?

Knock knock!
Who's there?
Walrus.
Walrus who?
Why do you
    walrus ask so
    many questions?

Knock knock!
Who's there?
Les.
Les who?
Les-sons to be learned!

Knock knock!
Who's there?
Garden.
Garden who?
Garden the secret treasure!

Knock knock!
Who's there?
Value.
Value who?
Value come to the park with me?

Knock knock!
Who's there?
Iona.
Iona who?
Iona TV set!

What's So Funny

Knock knock!
Who's there?
Burden.
Burden who?
Burden the tree
is singing!

Knock knock!
Who's there?
Dozen.
Dozen who?
Dozen anyone know who I am?

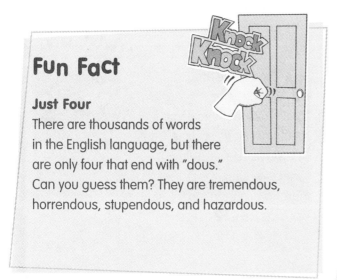

Fun Fact

Just Four

There are thousands of words in the English language, but there are only four that end with "dous." Can you guess them? They are tremendous, horrendous, stupendous, and hazardous.

Knock knock!
Who's there?
Disguise.
Disguise who?
Disguise the limit!

Knock knock!
Who's there?
Arf.
Arf who?
Arf-a-got!

Knock knock!
Who's there?
Hallways.
Hallways who?
Hallways running off somewhere!

Knock knock!
Who's there?
Oil.
Oil who?
Oil we do is tell knock-knock jokes!

Knock knock!
Who's there?
Irish.
Irish who?
I-rish I had lots of money!

Knock knock!
Who's there?
Tibet.
Tibet who?
Early Tibet,
   early to rise!

Knock knock!
Who's there?
Rex.
Rex who?
Rex-taurant's just down the road!

Knock knock!
Who's there?
Sadie.
Sadie who?
Sadie word and I'll be there!

Knock knock!
Who's there?
Dragon.
Dragon who?
Dragon your feet will
get you nowhere!

What am I?

When I strut around, I look very proud. My feathers come in different colors, and they make me very beautiful. When I dance around, my feathers spread out like a fan.
What am I?

A peacock

Knock knock!
Who's there?
Andover.
Andover who?
Andover the loot!

Knock knock!
Who's there?
Norton.
Norton who?
Norton nice to say!

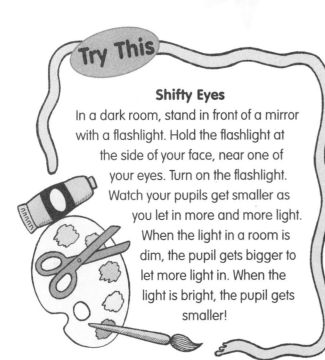

Try This

Shifty Eyes
In a dark room, stand in front of a mirror with a flashlight. Hold the flashlight at the side of your face, near one of your eyes. Turn on the flashlight. Watch your pupils get smaller as you let in more and more light. When the light in a room is dim, the pupil gets bigger to let more light in. When the light is bright, the pupil gets smaller!

Knock knock!
Who's there?
Roland.
Roland who?
Rol-and some milk would be nice!

Chapter 10
Knock Me Down, More Knock-Knocks

Knock knock!
Who's there?
Bea.
Bea who?
Bea cool!

Knock knock!
Who's there?
Dancer.
Dancer who?
'Dancer to the question!

Knock knock!
Who's there?
Tuna.
Tuna who?
Tuna your piano, it sounds horrible!

Knock knock!
Who's there?
Saturn.
Saturn who?
Saturn day is my favorite day of
    the week!

Knock knock!
Who's there?
Snow.
Snow who?
'Snow business like show business!

Knock knock!
Who's there?
Avon.
Avon who?
Avon-a go home!

What am I?

I live in the sea and have eight arms. I use all my arms to catch food. I'm squishy and when I'm in danger I release a cloud of black ink to scare off my enemies. **What am I?**

An octopus

What's So Funny

Knock knock!
Who's there?
Donavan.
Donavan who?
Donavan think
about leaving!

Knock knock!
Who's there?
Odysseus.
Odysseus who?
Odysseus the last time
   I'm going to tell you!

Knock knock!
Who's there?
Value.
Value who?
Value be my best friend?

Knock knock!
Who's there?
Morgan.
Morgan who?
Morgan you can hope for!

Knock knock!
Who's there?
Kenya.
Kenya who?
Kenya think of a new game?

Knock knock!
Who's there?
Discounts.
Discounts who?
Discounts toward your final grade!

Knock knock!
Who's there?
Howard.
Howard who?
And Howard you?

Knock knock!
Who's there?
Lenny.
Lenny who?
Lenny in the
house please!

Knock knock!
Who's there?
Amos.
Amos who?
Amos-quito
   just bit me!

Knock knock!
Who's there?
Sherwood.
Sherwood who?
Sherwood like to be invited in!

Knock knock!
Who's there?
Mac.
Mac who?
Mac and cheese!

Knock knock!
Who's there?
Toot and Teresa.
Toot and Teresa who?
Toots company, Teresa crowd!

Knock knock!
Who's there?
Ina Claire.
Ina Claire who?
Ina Claire night you can see the stars!

Knock knock!
Who's there?
Dustin.
Dustin who?
Dustin off the furniture!

Try This

Flower Power
Find a white flower with a long stem. Split the stem up the middle without breaking the flower. Get two glasses of water, and then add a few drops of food coloring to the water, using a different color for each glass. Put one of the stem halves in one glass, and the other half in the other glass. Now, just wait and watch the flower turn two different colors!

Who comes first?

Fill in the answers to the clues, placing one letter in each numbered space. Then transfer the letters to the boxes that have the same numbers. When all the boxes are filled in correctly, you will have the answer to the joke!

A. ___ ___ ___ ___ What a tree is made of.
   9   3   11   24

B. ___ ___ ___ Something to play with.
   5   8   32

C. ___ ___ ___ ___ ___ Having great weight.
   13   21   14   15   10

D. ___ ___ ___ ___ ___ To use the mind.
   34   26   1   4   6

E. ___ ___ ___ ___ ___ Shaped like a circle.
   31   19   12   22   28

F. ___ ___ ___ ___ Opposite of shallow.
   2   16   33   20

G. ___ ___ ___ ___ A short letter or message.
   17   29   25   23

H. ___ ___ ___ ___ A shade of color.
   18   30   7   27

KNOCK, KNOCK.

WHO'S THERE?

| 1D | | 2F | 3A | 4D | ' | 5B | | 6D | 7H | 8B | 9A |

| 10 C | 11 A | 12 E | | 13 C | 14 C | 15 C | 16 F | 17 G | ' | 18 H |

| 19 E | 20 F | 21 C | 22 E | 23 G | 24 A | | 25 G | 26 D | 27 H |

| 28 E | 29 G | 30 H | 31 E | | 32 B | 33 F | 34 D | ! |

Read My Lips

Color in each letter found in the word L-I-P-S. Then, write the remaining uncolored letters, in order, on the lines provided. When you're finished, you will have the answer to this joke:

Knock, knock.   **Who's there?**
Me.   **Me who?**

```
SLIPLIPSL
LDIOPNST
LIYIPOPUS
LKINPOSW
PLIPLSLIP
YLOIUPRS
ILOLWINP
SNLAIMPE
PLSLIPLSP
```

'
___ ___ ___

___ ___ ___ ?

Knock knock!
Who's there?
Nadia.
Nadia who?
Nadia head if you agree!

Knock knock!
Who's there?
Pond.
Pond who?
Pond a nail into the wall!

Knock knock!
Who's there?
Dodger.
Dodger who?
Dodger before she
   hits you with the ball!

ham actor:

A performer who likes a lot of attention while on stage. Ham actors love to show off by overacting and using exaggerated gestures.

118

Fun Fact

Meet the Hummingbird

Hummingbirds are very special birds. For one thing, they are the only birds that can fly backward. Some species of hummingbirds are also the smallest birds on the planet. The Bee Hummingbird is only about 2¼ inches long, and half of that is its beak and tail! Hummingbird species also have some exotic names, such as Glowing Puffleg, the Purple-Crowned Fairy, and the Glittering-Bellied Emerald.

Knock knock!
Who's there?
Adore.
Adore who?
Adore is open!

Knock knock!
Who's there?
Cotton.
Cotton who?
I've Cotton as far as I could!

Knock knock!
Who's there?
Armageddon.
Armageddon who?
Armageddon out of here!

Knock knock!
Who's there?
Gravy.
Gravy who?
Gravy Crockett!

Knock knock!
Who's there?
Bill.
Bill who?
Bill collector!

Knock knock!
Who's there?
Archie.
Archie who?
Archie-oo!

Knock knock!
Who's there?
Cot.
Cot who?
Cot you stealing the cookies!

Knock knock!
Who's there?
Falafel.
Falafel who?
Falafel about the fight!

Knock knock!
Who's there?
Sis.
Sis who?
'Sis any way to treat me?

Knock knock!
Who's there?
Belize.
Belize who?
Belize let me in!

Knock knock!
Who's there?
Combat.
Combat who?
Combat when you have something nice
to say!

Knock knock!
Who's there?
Hearsay.
Hearsay who?
Hearsay present for you!

Knock knock!
Who's there?
Bin.
Bin who?
Bin a nice visit!

What am I?

I live in a very small place all by myself. There are no doors or windows and I don't go outside. If I want to leave, I have to break down the walls.
What am I?

A baby chick waiting to hatch

Knock knock!
Who's there?
Ida.
Ida who?
I'da done it myself if I could!

Knock knock!
Who's there?
Ana.
Ana who?
Ana-conda is a scary snake!

Try This

Blowing in the Wind

On a windy day, wet your finger and hold it up in the air. You'll notice that one side of your finger feels colder than the other. This is because the wind made the water on that side of your finger evaporate quicker. This is a good way to tell which way the wind is blowing!

Tennis Anyone?

Look at the fraction below each blank. Pick the shape that shows that fraction, using these rules: The white part of each shape is empty; the shaded part is full. Write the letter that's near that shape on the line. When you are finished, you will have the answer to this joke:

Knock knock. Who's there? **Tennis.** Tennis who?

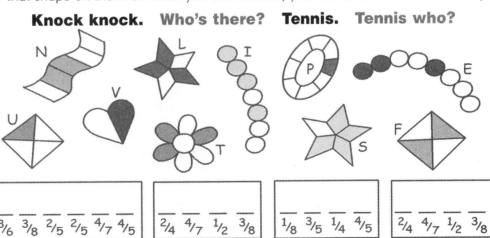

$\frac{3}{6}$ $\frac{3}{8}$ $\frac{2}{5}$ $\frac{2}{5}$ $\frac{4}{7}$ $\frac{4}{5}$ $\frac{2}{4}$ $\frac{4}{7}$ $\frac{1}{2}$ $\frac{3}{8}$ $\frac{1}{8}$ $\frac{3}{5}$ $\frac{1}{4}$ $\frac{4}{5}$ $\frac{2}{4}$ $\frac{4}{7}$ $\frac{1}{2}$ $\frac{3}{8}$!

Knock knock!
Who's there?
Firewood.
Firewood who?
Firewood go out late every night!

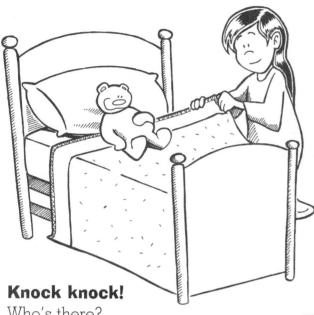

Knock knock!
Who's there?
Babylon.
Babylon who?
Babylon and on, that's all she does!

Knock knock!
Who's there?
India.
India who?
India nighttime I go to bed!

Knock knock!
Who's there?
Walt.
Walt who?
Walt till your mother gets home!

Knock knock!
Who's there?
Allison.
Allison who?
Al-lison to you when you speak!

What's So Funny

Knock knock!
Who's there?
Paul.
Paul who?
Paul's well that ends well!

Knock knock!
Who's there?
Faye.
Faye who?
Faye all laugh when I tell a joke!

slapstick:

A type of physical comedy with a lot of horseplay. The Three Stooges—Larry, Moe, and Curly—are famous for their slapstick routines. Slapstick is also used to describe an instrument made of two flat pieces of wood that are fastened together to make a striking sound. Sometimes comedians will use this instrument in their routines.

Words to Know

Knock knock!
Who's there?
Abby.
Abby who?
Abby stung me!

Knock knock!
Who's there?
Gibbon.
Gibbon who?
Gibbon me a hard time!

Knock knock!
Who's there?
Aunt Lou.
Aunt Lou who?
Aunt Lou do you think you are?

Knock knock!
Who's there?
Witches.
Witches who?
Witches the right way?

Knock knock!
Who's there?
Ben.
Ben who?
Ben knocking on the door all day!

Knock knock!
Who's there?
Ivana.
Ivana who?
Ivana go home!

Knock knock!
Who's there?
House.
House who?
House it going?

What am I?

I've been around for millions of years, yet I'm never more than a month old. Some people say I look like Swiss cheese. You'll hardly ever see me during the day! **What am I?**

The moon

Knock knock!
Who's there?
Shah.
Shah who?
Shah the door, it's cold outside!

Knock knock!
Who's there?
Greece.
Greece who?
Greece is all over the stove!

Knock knock!
Who's there?
Juicy.
Juicy who?
'Juicy what I see?

Knock knock!
Who's there?
Dawn.
Dawn who?
Dawn leave me, I'll miss you!

Knock knock!
Who's there?
Will.
Will who?
Will come home!

Knock knock!
Who's there?
Abbott.
Abbott who?
Ab-bott time you asked!

Fun Fact

Aren't You Glad You Know It?
The English language is very hard to learn. That's because there are so many special rules and so many words that sound the same but have completely different meanings. For example, if your throat hurts, you can be **hoarse**, but you can also go to the farm and ride a **horse**. Soldiers may **desert** the fort, but eat **dessert**.

Appendices

Appendix A: More Books to Read

Bayne, Kaitlyn Ruth. *Little Book of Knock Knock Jokes*. Lawrence Teacher Publishing Group, 2000. Knock-knocks on the go. Take this small book wherever you go and have a laughing good time all the time.

Birtles, Jasmine. *1001 Knock Knock Jokes*. Constable Robinson. 1998. Kids will be amused for hours with these funny bone–tickling knock-knocks.

Hall, Katy. *Back-to-School Belly Busters and Other Side-Splitting Knock-Knock Jokes That Are Too Cool for School*. HarperFestival, 2002. Something to make schooldays more interesting. Lift-up flaps and cutouts are all part of this enjoyable knock-knock book.

Hall, Katy. *Boo Who? And Other Wicked Halloween Knock-Knock Jokes*. HarperFestival, 2000. Get ready for some spine-tingling fun with these spooky Halloween jokes. It's truly fang-tastic.

Hall, Katy. *Olive You! And Other Valentine Knock-Knock Jokes You'll A-Door*. HarperFestival, 2000. This Valentine's Day knock-knock book will tickle you pink. Lift the flap to find the answers, and laugh out loud.

Hills, Tad. *Knock, Knock! Who's There? My First Book of Knock-Knock Jokes*. Little Simon, 2000. This delightful book will get any kid rolling with laughter. Pull-back flaps with colorful characters show how the knock-knock jokes use wordplay.

Keller, Charles. *Kids' Funniest Knock-Knocks*. Sterling Publications, 2001. Come along for a parade of knock-knock jokes. It's tons of fun with songs, food, animals, and names.

Keller, Charles. *The Little Giant Book of Knock-Knocks*. Sterling Publications, 1997. Arranged in alphabetical order, these knock-knocks come complete with zany cartoon drawings.

Kilgarriff, Michael. *1,000 Knock Knock Jokes for Kids*. Ballantine Books. 1990. This book is laugh-out-loud funny, and includes jokes about everything from names, songs, and animals to insults, sayings, and puns.

Phillips, Bob. *The World's Greatest Knock-Knock Jokes for Kids!* Harvest House Publishers, 2000. Laugh all day long as you read one great joke after another.

Appendix B: Web Sites You Can Visit

✐ www.azkidsnet.com/JSknockjoke.htm

Learn new knock-knock jokes by putting your computer mouse over "Who's There?" to see the question. Then put your mouse over "Answer" and get ready for a good laugh.

✐ www.ahajokes.com/knock_knock_jokes.html

This Web page will keep you busy for hours. There are more knock-knock jokes than you can imagine. They also are updated often so you can go back again and again.

✐ www.knock-knock-joke.com

Just how many knock-knock jokes are there? Well, this Web site tries to find out. There are hundreds of jokes to choose from.

✐ www.christmasjokes.co.uk/jokes/knock-knock.html

Everyone loves a good holiday joke. This Web site won't let you down. Find a ton of Christmas-related knock-knock jokes here.

✐ www.amazinghumor.com/jokes/knock-knockjokes/

This Web site gives you knock-knock jokes in alphabetical order. Just click on a letter and you'll be in for a real treat.

✐ www.owlkids.com/owl/owl_last_laugh.html

This Web site is sure to brighten your day. The jokes will keep you laughing and the brainteasers will keep you thinking all day long.

✐ http://pbskids.org

Head to this Web site for all-day activities. There are games, jokes, coloring activities, and a "Did You Know?" section. There also are tons of links for cool information.

✐ www.edbydesign.com/kidsact.html

Search this Web site for tons of interactive activities, including word scramblers and storytelling.

✐ www.yahooligans.com/content/jokes/

There are all kinds of jokes and games on this Web site to provide hours of fun. Just click on a joke to find the answer.

✐ www.niehs.nih.gov/kids/jokesknock.htm

Get ready for loads of fun! You'll just love all these brainteasers, riddles, and knock-knocks.

Appendix C: Glossary

absurd: Completely ridiculous or silly. For example, it is absurd to think that there is a man living on the moon.

comedian: A man or a woman who makes a living by being funny. It is a comedian's job to tell jokes and get people giggling.

comic relief: A funny moment in a play or show that breaks up a very serious scene. Comic relief comes just in the nick of time when everything seems to be very tense and just too serious.

funny bone: Ever hear someone say they are going to tickle your funny bone? Well, they aren't actually going to tickle a bone in your body. They mean they are going to make you laugh. Your funny bone is your sense of humor.

funnyman: A funnyman is just that, a man who is funny. Sometimes a comedian will be introduced to his audience with this title. One famous funnyman is Robin Williams. Of course, there are funny-women too!

gag: A prank or joke that makes people laugh. Sometimes a comedian will have a running gag in the show (that means the same gag will be repeated over and over again). Running gags can also be part of television shows, movies, and plays.

guffaw: A loud burst of uncontrollable laughter. If you're watching a movie that has many funny things happening, you might not be able to control your laughter. That's when you are likely to guffaw!

ham actor: A performer who likes a lot of attention while on stage. Ham actors love to show off by overacting and using exaggerated gestures.

hilarious: Something that makes you laugh so hard you can't control yourself. You just keep laughing and laughing. Anything or anyone can be hilarious!

jest: Not being serious. Sometimes a jest is a playful remark or a prank. In the Middle Ages, a jester was someone who worked at the king's court to entertain royalty.

palindrome: A word, sentence, or number that reads the same backward and forward. For example, the number 13531 is a palindrome. So is the name Bob.

parody: A play, sometimes a musical, that is meant to be very funny and often makes fun of something.

pun: A word or joke that is a play on words and may have two or more meanings. All knock-knock jokes are puns.

punch line: A punch line has nothing to do with anyone punching. It is actually the funniest—or punchiest—part of a joke. Usually the punch line comes at the end of the joke. Ever listen to a long joke only to find out that the punch line wasn't so funny after all? That's no fun!

shtick: A show-business word that means a comedian's routine. Most comedians have a certain type of act that they do much of the time. Comedians go on tour to do their shtick.

side-splitting: Have you ever laughed so hard you thought you'd just bust? That's where the term "side-splitting" comes from. Side-splitting laughter is the type of laughter that takes over your whole body.

skit: A short and funny play. A class might write a skit for a school performance. Sometimes a show will be made up of a few different skits.

slapstick: A type of physical comedy with a lot of horseplay. The Three Stooges—Larry, Moe, and Curly—are famous for their slapstick routines. Slapstick is also used to describe an instrument made of two flat pieces of wood that are fastened together to make a striking sound. Sometimes comedians will use this instrument in their routines.

spoof: A light and playful way of making fun of something. You might see a television show, a movie, or a play that's a spoof, or even read a story that spoofs something or someone.

vaudeville: A staged performance including a lot of different types of acts. There could be singing, dancing, comedy, acrobats, and even animal tricks. Everyone loves a good vaudeville show!

whimsical: Light or funny. Many things are whimsical. For example, knock-knock jokes are pretty whimsical! Stage-acting with a lot of clowning around is pretty whimsical too.

witty: Something that is clever or amusing. A witty statement will impress people or give them a good chuckle.

PUZZLE ANSWERS

page 5 • Noah

SURPRISE NOAH

DOESN'T KNOW YOU

EITHER

page 7 • Knocked to Pieces

K	N	O	C	K		K	N	O	C	K
W	H	O	'	S		T	H	E	R	E	?
		L	U	K	E		L	U	K	E
	W	H	O	?		L	U	K	E	
W	H	O		I	T		I	S		B	E
F	O	R	E		Y	O	U		O	P	E
N		T	H	E		D	O	O	R	!

page 8 • Say What?

ANSWER:
LENA
LITTLE
CLOSER
AND I
WILL
TELL YOU

page 8 • I Can't Hear You

page 16 • Mix and Match

KNOCK, KNOCK.
Who's there?
BOO.
Boo who?   ①

KNOCK, KNOCK.
Who's there?
CASH.
Cash who?   ④

KNOCK, KNOCK.
Who's there?
COWS.
Cows who?   ②

KNOCK, KNOCK.
Who's there?
ATCH.
Atch who?   ⑤

KNOCK, KNOCK.
Who's there?
YOU.
You who?   ⑥

KNOCK, KNOCK.
Who's there?
YA.
Ya who?   ③

page 21 • Please Fix That

P	O	O	D	L	E
L	I	T	T	L	E
	O	I	L		O	N
	T	H	A	T	
D	O	O	R		-
	I	T	'	S	
S	Q	U	E	A	K	Y

PUZZLE ANSWERS

page 24 • **Hidden Helper**

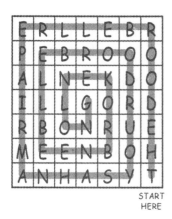

The doorbell repairman. Has your doorbell been broken long?

page 31 • **Alli-OOPS!**

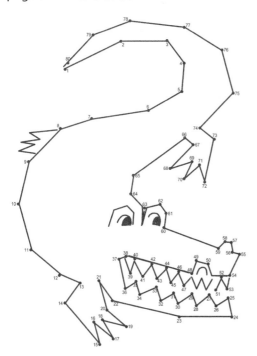

page 32 • **How Polite!**

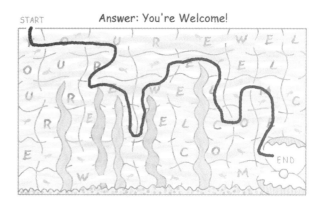

page 35 • **It's Me!**

A. K I T E S Paper toys flown by strings.
   15 3 14 20 13

B. S U M M E R Between spring and winter.
   1 12 19 11 6 4

C. W H Y For what reason?
   25 2 8

D. W O O L Y Covered in wool.
   18 9 17 5 22

E. N O U N A person, place, or thing.
   16 24 10 23

F. B Y Close to, or beside.
   21 7

1	2	3	4	5	6	7		8	9	10		11	12	13	14
S	H	I	R	L	E	Y		Y	O	U		M	U	S	T

15	16	17	18		19	20		21	22		23	24	25
K	N	O	W		M	E		B	Y		N	O	W	!

page 42 • **Which Window?**

ANSWER: Juan of your friends!

131

PUZZLE ANSWERS

page 47 • Half a Chance

E-4	Q-5	E+4	T-1	M+2	14
A	L	I	S	O	N

T+3	T-5	M+1	A+3	5	V-4	12	D-3	J+4	G-3
W	O	N	D	E	R	L	A	N	D

page 51 • Rhyme Time

FLOCK
CLOCK
WINDSOCK
SHOCK
LOCK
DOCK
SHAMROCK
SOCK
BLOCK
ROCK

page 55 • Crazy Criss-Cross

```
D E L I G H T E D
      M E R R Y
      F I N E
E X C I T E D
  W O N D E R F U L
    P E R K Y
    C H E E R F U L
A W E S O M E
      S W E L L
F A N T A S T I C
      G R E A T
  E X C E L L E N T
H A P P Y
    G O O D
    S U N N Y
```

page 58 • Knock Once

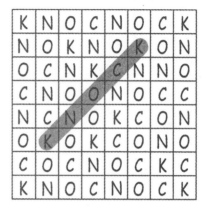

```
K N O C N O C K
N O K N O K O N
O C N K C N N O
C N O O N O C C
N C N O K C O N
O K O K C O N O
C O C N O C K C
K N O C N O C K
```

page 63 • Who Is It?

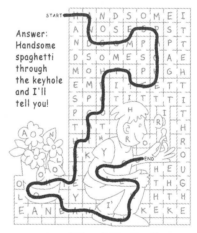

Answer: Handsome spaghetti through the keyhole and I'll tell you!

page 68 • Mixed Up Endings

1. **Knock, knock.** Who's there? **Who.** Who who?
   There's a terrible echo in here!

2. **Knock, knock.** Who's there? **Pecan.** Pecan who?
   Pecan somebody else next time!

3. **Knock, knock.** Who's there? **Cook.** Cook who?
   You sound like a Swiss clock!

4. **Knock, knock.** Who's there? **Anita.** Anita who?
   Anita minute to think it over!

5. **Knock, knock.** Who's there? **Kangar.** Kangar who?
   Yes, I'm from Australia!

6. **Knock, knock.** Who's there? **Little old lady.** Little old lady who?
   You can yodel?

PUZZLE ANSWERS

page 71 • **Wendy's Here**

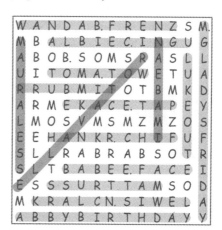

page 75 • **Open the Door**

1. <u>AXE</u> your sister who I am!

2. <u>WOODEN</u> <u>SHOE</u> like to know?

3. <u>CANE</u> you come out and play?

4. <u>DISHES</u> me! Who are you?

5. <u>TANK</u> you for for inviting me over!

6. <u>OWL</u> see you when you open the door!

7. <u>HOUSE</u> by you?

page 80 • **Come and Get It!**

G U S
W H O ' S
C O M I N G
T O
D I N N E R!

page 83 • **We Deliver!**

1. Knock, knock. Who's there? Manilla. Manilla who?
Manilla <u>I. Scream</u>

2. Knock, knock. Who's there? Barbie. Barbie who?
Barbie <u>Q. Chicken</u>

3. Knock, knock. Who's there? Frank. Frank who?
Frank <u>N. Beans</u>

4. Knock, knock. Who's there? Hamen. Hamen who?
Hamen <u>Eggs</u>

5. Knock, knock. Who's there? Roland. Roland who?
Roland <u>Butter</u>

6. Knock, knock. Who's there? Marsha. Marsha who?
Marsha <u>Mallow</u>

7. Knock, knock. Who's there? Sultan. Sultan who?
Sultan <u>Pepper</u>

page 86 • **Funny Friends**

```
W A N D A B . F R E N Z S M .
M B A L B I E C I N G U G
A B O B . S O M S R A S L L
U I T O M A . T O W E T U A
R R U B M I T O T B M K D
A R M E K A C E . T A P E Y
L M O S V M S M Z M Z O S
E E H A N K R . C H I F U F
S L L R A B R A B S O T R
S L T B A B E E . F A C E I
E S S U R T T A M S O D
M K R A L C N . S I W E L A
A B B Y B I R T H D A Y Y
```

page 92 • **Ho, Ho, Ho**

<u>O</u>h, y<u>ou</u> b<u>e</u>t<u>a</u> w<u>a</u>tch <u>ou</u>t,
y<u>ou</u> b<u>e</u>t<u>a</u> n<u>o</u>t cry,
y<u>ou</u> b<u>e</u>t<u>a</u> n<u>o</u>t p<u>ou</u>t,
I'm t<u>e</u>ll<u>i</u>ng y<u>ou</u> why —
S<u>a</u>nt<u>a</u> Cl<u>au</u>s <u>i</u>s c<u>o</u>m<u>i</u>ng
t<u>o</u> t<u>ow</u>n!

PUZZLE ANSWERS

page 95 • **Aye, Aye Captain**

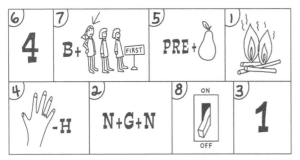

Fire engine one and prepare for blast off!

page 97 • **Where in the World?**

1. __ALASKA__ questions, you give the answers!
2. __WARSAW__ matter? Cat got your tongue?
3. __IRAN__ to the party!
4. __ARKANSAS__ lots of wood with my chain saw!
5. __KENYA__ come out and play?
6. __JAMAICA__ me very happy!
7. __HAVANA__ go home now!
8. __TIJUANA__ ride my bike?
9. __TAIWAN__ a puppy for Christmas!
10. __YUKON__ have it, I don't want it!

page 105 • **Do I Know You?, Puzzle 1**

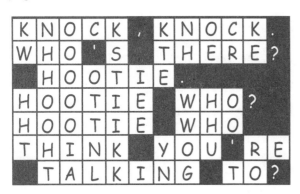

page 105 • **Do I Know You?, Puzzle 2**

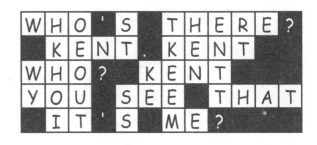

page 106 • **Don't Forget to Brush**

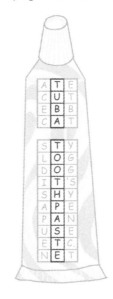

PUZZLE ANSWERS

page 108 • Dots Funny

NAD OYU OT
AND YOU TO

NIFD UOT!
FIND OUT

page 117 • Who Comes First?

A. $\underline{W}_9 \underline{O}_3 \underline{O}_{11} \underline{D}_{24}$ What a tree is made of.

B. $\underline{T}_5 \underline{O}_8 \underline{Y}_{32}$ Something to play with.

C. $\underline{H}_{13} \underline{E}_{21} \underline{A}_{14} \underline{V}_{15} \underline{Y}_{10}$ Having great weight.

D. $\underline{T}_{34} \underline{H}_{26} \underline{I}_1 \underline{N}_4 \underline{K}_6$ To use the mind.

E. $\underline{R}_{31} \underline{O}_{19} \underline{U}_{12} \underline{N}_{22} \underline{D}_{28}$ Shaped like a circle.

F. $\underline{D}_2 \underline{E}_{16} \underline{E}_{33} \underline{P}_{20}$ Opposite of shallow.

G. $\underline{N}_{17} \underline{O}_{29} \underline{T}_{25} \underline{E}_{23}$ A short letter or message.

H. $\underline{T}_{18} \underline{O}_{30} \underline{N}_7 \underline{E}_{27}$ A shade of color.

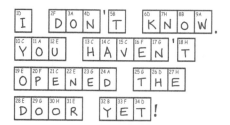

1D	2F	3A	4D	5B		6D	7H	8B	9A
I	D	O	N	T	'	K	N	O	W

10C	11A	12E		13C	14C	15C	16F	17G		18H
Y	O	U		H	A	V	E	N	'	T

19E	20F	21C	22E	23G	24A		25G	26D	27H
O	P	E	N	E	D		T	H	E

28E	29G	30H	31E		32B	33F	34D
D	O	O	R		Y	E	T	!

page 118 • Read My Lips

DON'T YOU KNOW
YOUR OWN NAME?

page 121 • Tennis Anyone?

$\underline{T}_{3/6} \underline{E}_{3/8} \underline{N}_{2/5} \underline{N}_{2/5} \underline{I}_{4/7} \underline{S}_{4/5}$ $\underline{F}_{2/4} \underline{I}_{4/7} \underline{V}_{1/2} \underline{E}_{3/8}$

$\underline{P}_{1/8} \underline{L}_{3/5} \underline{U}_{1/4} \underline{S}_{4/5}$ $\underline{F}_{2/4} \underline{I}_{4/7} \underline{V}_{1/2} \underline{E}_{3/8}$!

THE EVERYTHING®

KIDS'

SERIES!

Packed with tons of information, activities, and puzzles, the Everything® Kids' books are perennial bestsellers that keep kids active and engaged. Each book is 8" x 9 1/4", 144 pages, and two-color throughout.

All this at the incredible price of $6.95!

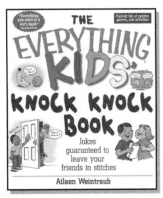

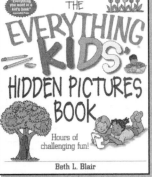

The Everything® Kids' Knock
Knock Book
1-59337-127-6 ($9.95 CAN)

The Everything® Kids' Hidden
Pictures Book
1-59337-128-4 ($9.95 CAN)

The Everything® Kids' Baseball Book, 3rd Ed.
  1-59337-070-9

The Everything® Kids' Bible Trivia Book
  1-59337-031-8

The Everything® Kids' Bugs Book
  1-58062-892-3

The Everything® Kids' Christmas Puzzle &
  Activity Book
  1-58062-965-2

The Everything® Kids' Cookbook
  1-58062-658-0

The Everything® Kids' Halloween Puzzle &
  Activity Book
  1-58062-959-8

The Everything® Kids' Joke Book
  1-58062-686-6

The Everything® Kids' Math Puzzles Book
  1-58062-773-0

The Everything® Kids' Mazes Book
  1-58062-558-4

The Everything® Kids' Money Book
  1-58062-685-8 ($11.95 CAN)

The Everything® Kids' Monsters Book
  1-58062-657-2

The Everything® Kids' Nature Book
  1-58062-684-X ($11.95 CAN)

The Everything® Kids' Puzzle Book
  1-58062-687-4

The Everything® Kids' Riddles & Brain Teasers Book
  1-59337-036-9

The Everything® Kids' Science Experiments Book
  1-58062-557-6

The Everything® Kids' Soccer Book
  1-58062-642-4

The Everything® Kids' Travel Activity Book
  1-58062-641-6

All Kids' titles are priced at $6.95 ($10.95 CAN) unless otherwise noted.

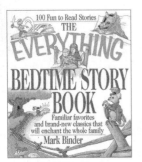

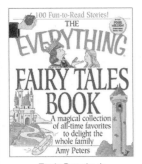